WHAT'S BOTHERING RASHI?

A GUIDE TO
IN-DEPTH ANALYSIS OF
HIS TORAH COMMENTARY

WHAT'S BOTHERING RASHI?

A GUIDE TO
IN-DEPTH ANALYSIS OF
HIS TORAH COMMENTARY

AVIGDOR
BONCHEK

SHEMOS

FOCUS ON RASHI—RAMBAN DISPUTES

JERUSALEM FELDHEIM PUBLISHERS NEW YORK

Published in collaboration with
Be'er HaTorah Institute

First published 1999
ISBN 0-87306-906-4

FELDHEIM PUBLISHERS
200 Airport Executive Park
Nanuet, NY 10954

POB 35002 / Jerusalem, Israel

Printed in Israel

Designed & Produced by:
Laser Pages Publishing Ltd., Jerusalem
972-2-6522226

בס"ד

שמואל קמנצקי
Rabbi S. Kamenetsky

2018 Upland Way
Philadelphia, Pa 19131

Home: 215-473-2798
Study: 215-473-1212

Rabbi Nachman Bulman
Yeshivat Ohr Somayach
Ohr Lagolah

הרב נחמן בולמן
ישיבת אור שמח
אור לגולה

בס"ד

כד' בניסן תשנ"ז
May 1, 1997

The writer of these lines has seen a notable new work on Rashi — "What's Bothering Rashi? A Guide to In-Depth Analysis of Rashi's Torah Commentary" by Avigdor Bonchek.

Students of Rashi are uniquely affected by his elemental simplicity of style. Children are indelibly stirred by his words, masters of Torah see in his words the heights of Torah genius. Over the centuries C'lal Yisroel sees Rashi as our companion in the eternal climb to Sinai. Commentary on Rashi has been as limitless as our people's preoccupation with Torah.

Central to the Torah revival of our time has therefore also been Rashi-commentary in English — except for one characteristic of classical Rashi learning; namely that Rashi learning "put us" as it were into his laboratory. We asked with him, we probed with him, we lived his solution. He took us to Sinai again with him.

R. Bonchek's work again takes us, as it were, into Rashi's cheder and Beis HaMedrash. He puts "us into Rashi" and not just "Rashi into us." Many will be grateful to him for his guide to learning Rashi.

Nachman Bulman

Rabbi Nachman Bulman

137/21 Ma'alot Daphna, Jerusalem 97762 Israel • Tel: 02-824321 :טל • 97762 ירושלים 137\21 מעלות דפנה

Dedication

This work is dedicated to the memory of
our beloved parents

Sam & Frieda Bonchek ע״ה
חנוך שלמה ב״ר משה שמואל הכהן ע״ה
פרימט בת ר׳ יצחק הכהן ע״ה

in love, respect and a profound sense of gratitude

Their children
Avigdor Bonchek & Mil Rothschild
and grandchildren

Dedication

SHUBERT SPERO

בס"ד

שמעון אלעזר הלוי ספירו

5 MENDELE APT. 16
JERUSALEM 92147 ISRAEL
TEL+FAX (02) 5639622

Sam Bonchek and Frieda Grossman, both born in Cleveland Ohio in the first decade of the twentieth century, were children of immigrants from Lomza, Poland and Fristik, Galicia. Frieda's father was a Zanzer *chasid* who served as a *shochet* and was held in great esteem by the Cleveland community. Sam's father was a businessman from a family known for its Jewish scholarship. His ways of pleasantness were admired by all who knew him. Sam and Frieda's home environments were rich in Jewish tradition and instilled in each of them a pride in their Jewishness and love for their tradition that was to stay with them all their lives.

Sam and Frieda married in 1927. Sam, a business man specialized in providing equipment for the physically handicapped, while Frieda was a housewife and אשת חיל in the full sense of the term. Together they brought up their two children, Mildred and Victor, to be committed and proud Jews.

However, in Cleveland of the 1940's, providing your children with an adequate Jewish education meant building the needed institutions from scratch. And that is precisely what Sam and Frieda set out to do. Together with a handful of others, they were instrumental in building a Jewish Day school, the Hebrew Academy; in bringing to Cleveland the Telshe Yeshiva, a world-reknown institution; in building the first community *mikveh* and in creating a vibrant Young Israel *kehillah*. Sam served on many important Federation committees. As chairman of the *kashrut* committee he revamped the entire *kashrut* system in the city, giving it a validity and respect that it had lacked. As a member of the acceptance committee for the Orthodox Old Age Home, he would personally visit the homes of elderly candidates to give them a personal welcome, making them feel wanted and respected thus easing the difficult transition into their new surroundings.

Sam was מעורב עם הבריאות. He had an ebullent personality, was outgoing, articulate and had an engaging sense of humor. He was the perfect "organization man" — raising funds, generating enthusiasm and getting people to volunteer. Frieda was kind, a woman of integrity who possessed a wisdom that saw through facades and triviality. Sam died at the young age of 52, at the height of his communal work. After his death Frieda continued, on her own, her quiet *chesed* activities. She passed away in Israel at the age of 92, after a long illness.

דוד לדור ישבח מעשיך וגבורתך יגידו.
יהי זכרם ברוך

Shubert Spero
Rabbi, Young Israel of Cleveland , 1950-1983

CONTENTS

* Ramban comments on Rashi

* Ramban comments on Rashi

Acknowledgments

מודה אני

"Acknowledgments" has a honored place in the annals of book publishing. For Jews it can be considered the literary equivalent of the מודה אני. The Hebrew word מודה means both "to thank" and "to acknowledge". For to express thanks is to acknowledge one's indebtedness. Following is my מודה אני, my acknowledgments and my expressions of gratitude, for the help and support I have received while working on this book.

First and foremost my gratitude to *Hashem* for planting in my mind and nurturing in my soul the interest to pursue this work on Rashi's classic Torah commentary. I feel privileged to be able to spend my free time in such a spiritually gratifying and intellectually stimulating way. To make the transition from enticing idea to "hard copy," from plan to published book, one needs all those "little things in life" that we take for granted — health, peace (living in Israel, that is not a casual state of affairs), and a supportive home environment.

For the former, I am grateful to *Hashem*; for the latter, to my wife, Shulamis. She has always been there for me and is an untiringly devoted mother to our children. Shulamis, שתחיה, has enthusiastically supported my work, even though the preparation of this book has taken up most of my "after-work" hours for the past several years. She was witness to the transformation of my interest in Rashi, as it developed from part-time pastime into consuming obsession. This inevitably impacted on her and on our life together. Under such circumstances her encouragement and emotional support were all the more needed and, for that reason, I am all the more grateful to her. She also had a direct hand in the preparation of this volume. She reviewed the manuscript several times and was instrumental in improving its grammatical and stylistic dimensions.

Our children, Chanoch, Elisheva, Yehoshua, Michal, Shira and Avi, שיחיו, themselves no slouches in Torah interpretation, were frequently the objects of my preoccupation and served as the sounding board for many of the ideas that went into the preparation of this book. They too offered helpful insights and constructive criticism. To them (and for them) I am thankful.

Rabbi Yitzchak Frank, my *chavrusah*, and I frequently discussed the Rashi and Ramban interpretations cited in this volume. I am happy to express my thanks to him for his insights which often helped clarify points that were unclear to me.

My mother, Frieda Bonchek, ע״ה passed away during the preparation of this volume."Part of her praise" is expressed in this volume's Dedication to her and to my father, ע״ה. I am sorry that she and my father didn't live to see these fruits of their fruits.

Publishing a book requires Zevuluns as well as Yisachars, financial supporters as well those who prepare the work itself. I am grateful to the friends and family, the Zevuluns, who made it possible for me to publish this work. My sister, Mil Rothschild, her children — my nieces and nephews — and my cousins, contributed generously. I am most indebted them, I truly appreciate their help in this endeavor.

It is my hope that this volume will be of benefit to all those who love the study of the Torah. Those who strive to uncover its manifold meanings, it spiritual lessons, and its moral and ethical teachings. Understanding Rashi's ever- fascinating commentary in all its depth, is a fitting starting point on that breathtaking journey.

Avigdor Bonchek

Jerusalem, 5759

A Fore Word

This book, *What's Bothering Rashi? Shemos*, is the second volume of a planned five volume work on Rashi's Torah commentary. The express purpose of these books is to illustrate a method of analysis of Rashi's commentary which enables one to derive maximum meaning from Rashi's words in his exquisitely precise commentary. The *Breishis* volume offered many examples of Rashi's basic exegetic style. This volume continues the application of that approach to Rashi's commentary on the Book of Exodus. In the first volume, I included a chapter introducing the student to Rashi's style and method of interpretation. That introduction is relevant for understanding our approach in this volume, as well. The student is advised to read that chapter before he starts this volume.

In order to expand the student's appreciation of the depth of Rashi's commentary, I have included in this volume a selection of disputes between Rashi and the Ramban.

From these examples we get a glimpse of the work of these two Torah geniuses, their individual styles, how they approach and analyze the words of the Torah. As an introduction to these disputes I have included an introductory chapter "Appreciating the Ramban."

APPRECIATING THE RAMBAN

Rashi (1040–1104) and the Ramban (1194–1274) are the giants of Torah commentary. Each in his own way has broadened and deepened the meaning of the Written Law and through their commentaries have revealed the splendor which lies beneath its surface. Their styles of commentary are different; their impact on the Jewish people, similar. Both have generated love and veneration for the sublime wisdom and beauty of the Torah.

The Ramban wrote his Torah commentary about 150 years after Rashi wrote his. Rashi lived in Northern France at the beginning of the crusades. The Ramban lived in Spain in a hostile Christian environment. They represented different learning traditions, Rashi the North European, Ashkenasic tradition; the Ramban, the Spanish Sephardic tradition, each with its unique style of learning. Yet, in spite of their differences, they converge in their individual efforts to explain the *p'shat* and *drash* of the Torah. The Ramban was amongst the first Spanish scholars to be cognizant of, appreciate and relate to, the Northern European Torah scholarship, and to Rashi's commentary in particular. The Ramban held Rashi and his commentary in the highest regard. He writes the following in his poetic introduction:

> I will place for my enlightenment, the lights of the pure candelabrum
> The commentaries of our teacher, Shlomo [Rashi], . . .
> To him is the Right of the Firstborn . . .
> And with [his words] we will have discussions, investigations and
>   examinations
> In his *p'shat* and *drash* and every difficult *aggada*
> Which are mentioned in his commentaries.

In fact, one could say that the Ramban's Torah commentary is, at its core, a commentary on Rashi's commentary. In over 150 places in his commentary, the Ramban relates to Rashi's commentary.

In comparing the styles of commentary of these two prominent commentators, we can say, in brief, that Rashi's comments are usually short and focused, while the Ramban's are usually long and panoramic in their sweep. For a fuller discussion of Rashi's style of Torah commentary see my chapter "Appreciating Rashi" in the Bereishis volume of *"What's Bothering Rashi?"*

The popularity of Rashi's commentary is due in no small measure to his magical blend of *p'shat*, pithy aphorisms and inspiring *midrash*. But another factor which adds to its universal acceptance is his "bite-size" comments, which makes them easily digestible. All students learn *Chumash* with Rashi; few, on the other hand, are ever formally taught *Chumash* with Ramban. From the neophyte student to the scholarly Talmudist, all can find meaning, message and challenge in Rashi's commentary. The Ramban, on the other hand, is more difficult to understand, even on a superficial reading. Add to this the inclusion of kabbalistic interpretations in his commentary, and we can understand why his commentary never swept along as many adherents as did Rashi's. Yet, for all that, he remains the second most respected Torah commentator, after Rashi. We will discuss some characteristics of the Ramban's Torah commentary and how they differ from those of Rashi.

RASHI'S AND RAMBAN'S GOALS IN THEIR TORAH COMMENTARY _____

Rashi and the Ramban approach the task of commentary with different goals, as can be seen from their introductory comments. While the Ramban has an elaborate introduction to his commentary in both prose and poetry, Rashi has no introduction as such. The few words he does tell us about his agenda are slipped in, almost surreptitiously, into the body of his commentary. Let us compare them.

Rashi's famous statement about his exegetic purpose comes from his comment on Genesis 3:8. There he writes:

> **וישמעו.** יש מדרשי אגדה רבים וכבר סדרום רבותינו על מכונם בבראשית רבה ובשאר מדרשות ואני לא באתי אלא לפשוטו של מקרא ולאגדה המישבת דברי המקרא דבר דבור על אופניו.
>
> **And they heard**: There many *midrashei aggadah* and our Rabbis have already arranged them in their place in *Bereishis Rabbah* and other *midrashim*. But I have only come [to offer] the Plain Meaning of the Scriptures(פשוטו של מקרא) and the *aggadah* that fits in with words, each word in its place.

The Ramban, on the other hand, has a long introduction. He explains his specific purpose in writing his commentary:

"I will conduct myself as the custom of the early scholars to comfort the mind of the students who are weary of the exile and their vicissitudes who regularly read from the sedra on the Sabbaths and the Holidays, to attract their hearts with Plain Sense interpretations and some pleasant matters to those who are familiar with the hidden wisdom....There are new insights in our commentary in *p'shat* and the *midrashim*..."

We can see from our brief comparison that Rashi stresses *p'shat* and only those *midrashim* which have some textual basis, while the Ramban mentions his intention to offer new insights in the various realms of *p'shat*, *midrash* and *kabbalah*.

DIFFERENT STYLES IN COMMENTARY

The different styles of Rashi and Ramban are apparent right from the start. As we examine their very first comments to the first verse in the Torah we can already get a sense of their individual orientations.

Rashi's first comment is well known.

> **בראשית**: אמר ר׳ יצחק לא היה צריך להתחיל את התורה אלא מהחודש הזה לכם, שהיא מצוה ראשונה שנצטוו ישראל. ומה טעם פתח בבראשית...
>
> **In the beginning**: Rashi: Rav Yitzchak said: The Torah should have begun with the verse "This month shall be for you [the first month]" (Exodus 12:1), it being the first mitzvah that the Israelites were commanded. Why then does the Torah begin with "In the beginning"? etc.

The Ramban also comments on this verse. He begins immediately by quoting Rashi and then says:

> "This is an *Aggadah* which our teacher Shlomo [Rashi] wrote in his commentary. But one could ask regarding it: Indeed there is a great need to begin the Torah with 'In the beginning G-d created' because this is the root of our faith. He who does not believe in this and thinks that the world is eternal (i.e. was never created) is a denier of the main [tenet of Jewish belief] and he has no [part in] the Torah. The answer is etc."

This is an excellent example of the differing views of these two Torah commentators. Their disagreement here illustrates two basic differences in their view of the Torah and its interpretation.

First, by asking why the Torah does not begin with the first commandment to the Israelites, Rashi makes it clear that he views the Torah essentially as a book of commandments. A guide to Jewish living. Such a guide should logically begin with those commandments addressed to the recipients of the Torah, the people of Israel.

The Ramban, on the other hand, questions and analyzes Rav Yitzchak's assumption:

"Indeed there is great need to begin with 'In the beginning' since it is the root of our faith." From his question it is apparent that the Ramban views the Torah, not only as a book of *mitzvos*, but also as a compendium of basic Jewish beliefs. In this view, the creation story is an essential and integral part of the Torah, since it conveys a basic tenet of Jewish belief. Because of this orientation, the Ramban made his Torah commentary a treasure chest of essays elaborating the Torah's view on a multitude of issues, something you generally will not find in Rashi's commentary.

A second fundamental difference between Rashi and the Ramban that can also be seen in this first dispute, is in their approach to *midrash* interpretation. Typically Rashi in his commentary will quote a *midrash* without elaboration. He may change a word or two depending on the purpose of the particular comment, but he will not attempt a deeper interpretation of the message of the *midrash*.

The Ramban, on the other hand, does not accept *midrashim* at face value. He seeks a deeper understanding. In our verse he interprets the question of Rav Yitzchak in the *midrash*, in the following way: He asks: Why begin the Torah with the creation story, not because it is extraneous to the Torah's purpose, but because it is, in the final analysis, beyond human comprehension. We cannot possibly understand the creation *ex nihilo*, nor can we make sense of the meaning of the six days of creation from the Torah's minimal description. Only by learning personally from a teacher who himself has received his knowledge directly from the previous generations, says the Ramban, can any human attempt to comprehend the esoteric truths involved in the creation story. The meaning of Rav Yitzchak's question is, therefore, why begin with the Creation, its inclusion is superfluous. The Torah could just as well have begun with the *mitzvos*, among them the *mitzvah* of the Sabbath which contains a statement of the Divine creation of the world. In this way we would have been made aware of the essential concept of Divine creation, which, in the final analysis, is all we can ever possibly understand.

We see how the Ramban interprets the same words of Rav Yitzchak taken from the *midrash* very differently from Rashi. We can take it as axiomatic that in his Torah commentary the Ramban will analyze a *midrash*; and in so doing he brings his creative genius and original insights to his interpretation of *midrashim*.

Let us see another example where Rashi quotes a *midrash* and the Ramban breathes life into it. This example is from the story of Joseph, when, at Jacob's behest, he went to find his brothers in Shechem.

Genesis 37:15

וַיִּמְצָאֵהוּ אִישׁ וְהִנֵּה תֹעֶה בַּשָּׂדֶה וַיִּשְׁאָלֵהוּ הָאִישׁ לֵאמֹר מַה תְּבַקֵּשׁ.

וימצאהו איש: זה גבריאל, שנאמר יוהאיש גבריאל.

And a man found him: Rashi. This was the angel Gabriel. as it is said (Dan. 10:21) 'and the man Gabriel.'

Rashi makes this comment because he notes that the Torah takes the trouble to tell us an apparently insignificant incident, i.e. that Joseph got lost and a stranger found him and directed him to his brothers.

Let us see what the Ramban does with this *midrash*.

"The verse is stating that he [Joseph] was straying from the road not knowing where to go, and he entered a field, since he was looking for them in a place of pasture. *Scripture mentions this at length* in order to relate that many events befell him which could properly have caused him to return, but he endured everything patiently in respect for his father. It also informs us that the Divine decree is true and man's efforts are worthless. The Holy One, blessed be He, sent him an unwitting guide in order to bring him into their [the brothers] hands. It is this which the Sages intended when they said that these men were angels, for these events did not occur without purpose but rather to teach us "the counsel of *Hashem* will endure."

Let us analyze this beautifully insightful and instructive Ramban-comment to savor its full wisdom.

The Ramban does here what is typical of his commentary throughout. While paying close attention to the textual detail (*p'shat*), he views the events from a larger philosophical perspective. Notice how he explains Joseph's "straying in the field" since he was searching for his brothers who were with sheep, they would most likely be found in a field.

By saying "Scripture mentions this at length", the Ramban is emphasizing that the Torah is recounting these events, which appear to be trivial, for a deeper purpose than simple narrative detail. We should ask: What is the Torah's point in going into such detail about Joseph's difficulties in reaching his brothers? In fact, the only thing important here was that eventually he found them and then they threw him in a pit and in the end sold him into slavery.

His answer: The lesson from these details is that G-d's plan will inevitably be fulfilled. He wanted Joseph sold into slavery and this would be accomplished even if he got lost on the way. G-d would make sure that Joseph reached his destination by having an "innocent bystander" redirect Joseph to his brothers. The Ramban's unusual insight here is that the bystander is an ordinary person who himself isn't aware of the import of his actions. All is being guided from above. This human bystander is the "angel" which the Sages referred to, since he is, unbeknownst to himself, in the service of G-d's plan.

Note how the Ramban, like Rashi, bases his comment on the *midrash* which sees "the man" as an angel. But the Ramban's view of the angel in this case, is quite different from what we would have thought, had we taken the *midrash* at face value. This "angel" here was human, an apparent passerby. He gained the status of "angel" due the fact that he was in the right place at the right time all of which was orchestrated by Divine will; he was there to implement G-d's plan, as is the task of angels.

PSYCHOLOGICAL ELEMENTS IN RAMBAN'S COMMENTARY

A surprising discovery in the Ramban's commentary are his profound psychological insights. The depth of his insights is surprising because they were written hundreds of years before modern psychological theory.

Let us see how the Ramban uses psychological insight to interpret a *midrash*.

Leviticus 9:7

וַיֹּאמֶר מֹשֶׁה אֶל אַהֲרֹן קְרַב אֶל הַמִּזְבֵּחַ וַעֲשֵׂה אֶת חַטָּאתְךָ וְגוֹ׳

Following is Rashi's comment on this verse.

קְרַב אֶת הַמִּזְבֵּחַ. שֶׁהָיָה אַהֲרֹן בּוֹשׁ וְיָרֵא לָגֶשֶׁת אָמַר לוֹ מֹשֶׁה לָמָּה אַתָּה בּוֹשׁ? לְכָךְ נִבְחַרְתָּ!

Go near the alter. *Rashi*: For Aaron was diffident and feared to go near. Moses said to him, "Why are you diffident? For this purpose have you been chosen!"

The Ramban cites the full *midrash* which is the basis of Rashi's comment.

> "Our Rabbis have suggested a parable. This is similar to a king who married a woman and she was embarrassed in front of him. Her sister came to her and said: sister why have you entered [into marriage] if not to serve the king! Embolden yourself and go serve the king. So said Moses to Aaron, 'My brother, why were you chosen to be the High Priest if not to serve the L-rd. Embolden yourself and go do your service.' And some say that Aaron saw the altar in the image of an ox (calf). He was fearful of it. Moses entered and said: 'My brother Aaron, don't be afraid of what you are afraid. Embolden yourself and approach the altar.' Now the meaning of this is that since Aaron was the holy one of G-d and he had no sin other than that of the golden calf, that sin was constantly on his mind, as it says (Psalms 51:5) 'My sin is in front of me always.' It seemed to him that he saw the image of a calf interfering with his atonement. Therefore he (Moses) said to him, "Embolden yourself, don't be so lowly of spirit, for G-d has accepted your actions.'"

In the Ramban's view of this *midrash*, we are told that Aaron mentally projected his guilt feelings onto the altar in the imagery of a calf. This is truly an original psychological interpretation, some 600 years before modern depth-psychology discovered the concept of projection. Here too we see a characteristic of the Ramban's Torah commentary. He will frequently draw upon psychological factors in his interpretation of *p'shat* and *midrash*. When we compare this to Rashi's comment on the same verse, we see clearly the difference between the two. Rashi makes a statement based on the *midrash*; the Ramban elaborates with a depth interpretation of the *midrash*.

"THE SCRIPTURAL TEXT CANNOT LOSE ITS PLAIN MEANING"

The Talmud has a well known statement regarding the place of *p'shat* in Torah interpretation. It tells us (Tractate Shabbos 63a) that אין מקרא יוצא מידי פשוטו. No interpretation of a verse can supplant its Plain Meaning. This alerts the Torah commentator that he can never ignore the *p'shat*, no matter what other type of interpretation he offers. The Ramban, in his commentary on the Rambam's *Book of Mitzvos* (in his discussion of the Second Principle) makes an important comment in this respect. He clarifies the idea that verses in the Torah can have multiple meanings, all of which are valid. He says: "The [Sages] said 'The Scripture cannot lose its Plain Meaning'; they did not say 'The Scripture has only its Plain Meaning.' Rather the verse can bear two meanings and both can be true."

By this statement, the Ramban means that the Torah's meanings are multi-layered; the words of the Scripture bear many different types and many levels of interpretation. While this idea is accepted by all Torah commentators, the Ramban not only makes the idea explicit, he also builds the bulk of his commentary on this principle. He frequently offers several different interpretations, *p'shat*, *drash*, and *kabbalah*, all revolving on the same words of the Torah. He is fully cognizant of this multi-interpretative aspect of the Torah. He sees the various interpretations not as alternative explanations of the text, but rather as parallel meanings, each correct in its own realm of interpretation.

"THE TORAH IS NOT NECESSARILY IN CHRONOLOGICAL SEQUENCE"

Biblical commentators occasionally rely on the Talmudic axiom that the sequence of verses and events in the Torah are not always in chronological order. The Talmudic phrase is אין מוקדם ומאוחר בתורה. This is the last of Rav Eliezer ben Yose's Thirty Two Principles of *Midrashic* Interpretation, which are printed in the back of the volume containing the Tractate *Berachos*.

Rashi and Ramban relate to this principle in very different ways. Rashi will often refer to this principle in order to explain the order of events in the Torah, and in so doing, he changes their order from the way they are sequenced in the Torah. The Ramban, on the other hand, forcefully opposes the frequent application of this principle. He feels the Torah was written in chronological order except where the text clearly says otherwise. An example of such an exceptional case can be found in the first chapters in the Book of Numbers. Chapter 1 begins on the first day of the *second month* of the second year after the Exodus, while later on in chapter 9:1 the Torah records events that occurred previous to that, in the *first month* of the second year. Here there is no escaping the conclusion that "the Torah is not in chronological sequence." But, otherwise, in most cases, the Ramban makes great efforts to explain events so that their chronological order follows closely that of the biblical record.

An example of their different approaches can be found in their dispute regarding the chronological relationship between G-d's command to build the Tabernacle and the sin of the Golden Calf at Sinai. There we find the following Rashi:

וַיִּתֵּן אֶל מֹשֶׁה כְּכַלֹּתוֹ לְדַבֵּר אִתּוֹ בְּהַר סִינַי שְׁנֵי לֻחֹת הָעֵדֻת לֻחֹת אֶבֶן כְּתֻבִים בְּאֶצְבַּע אֱלֹקִים.

וַיִּתֵּן אֶל מֹשֶׁה. אין מוקדם ומאוחר בתורה – מעשה העגל קודם לצווי מלאכת המשכן ימים רבים היה, שהרי בי״ז בתמוז נשברו הלוחות וביום הכיפורים נתרצה הקב״ה לישראל. ולמחרת התחילו בנדבת המשכן והוקם באחד בניסן.

And He gave to Moses: *Rashi*: There is no "earlier" or "later" in the Torah — The event of the [Golden] Calf (Exodus Ch. 32) preceded the command to build the Tabernacle (Exodus Ch. 25) by many days. For on the seventeenth of Tamuz the Tablets were broken, and on Yom Kippur G-d was reconciled with Israel, and on the morrow they began with the donations for the Tabernacle and it was erected on the first of Nisan.

WHAT IS RASHI SAYING ?

Rashi is pointing out that the Golden Calf episode, which was made on the seventeenth of Tamuz (the fourth month after the Exodus), and is recorded in the Torah in Exodus, chapter 32, occurred before the events and commands regarding the building of the Tabernacle. The latter did not occur until several months later, "on the morrow of Yom Kippur" yet they are recorded in the Torah earlier, in chapter 25. The completion of the Tabernacle was on the first of Nisan, a half year later, nearly a year after the Exodus, and is recorded in the Torah in Leviticus 9:1 (see Rashi *ad loc.*). The Torah, on the other hand, records the sin of the Golden Calf *after* the command to make the Tabernacle and before its actual building. We see clearly that according to Rashi, the events did not occur in the order that they are recorded in the Torah.

The Ramban opposes Rashi's view. He expresses his opposition later, at the beginning of *parashas Vayakhel* (35:1). The Ramban is quite explicit about his opinion on the chronology of these events. There he writes:

"It is possible that on the day following his [Moses'] descent from the mountain that he told them the subject of the Tabernacle *which had been previously commanded before the breaking of the Tablets.* For since the Holy One blessed be He, became reconciled with them and gave Moses the second Tablets and also made a new covenant that G-d would go with them. He thereby returned to His previous relationship with them, and to the love of their 'wedding' and it was obvious that His Presence would be in their midst just as He had commanded him at first. Even as He said 'And let them make Me a Sanctuary that I may dwell amongst them.' (25:8) Therefore Moses now commanded them all that he had been told at first."

What Is the Ramban Saying?

The Ramban is explaining the sequence of events — G-d's command to build the Tabernacle, (Exodus Ch. 25); the sin of the Golden Calf, (Exodus Ch. 32); G-d's reconciliation with the Children of Israel, (Exodus Ch. 33:14); and finally the construction of the Tabernacle (Exodus Ch. 36) in the order they are recorded in the Torah. He has no need to rearrange the order of the verses as Rashi does.

The Theological Implication of the Dispute

The different views of Rashi and the Ramban regarding the timing of G-d's command to build the Tabernacle is not just an issue of history and chronology; the dispute has theological significance. It would seem that Rashi views the Tabernacle as a necessary *mitzvah* which was a consequence of the fact that the Israelites sinned. It offered them a vehicle for repentance. The conclusion would seem to be that had there been no Golden Calf, there would have been no Tabernacle. In an ideal state, there would be no need for one.

The Ramban, on the other hand, says the idea of the Tabernacle came before, and is unrelated to, the sin of the Golden Calf. It's purpose is not exclusively for repentance, it goes beyond that. As David said "As for me, nearness to G-d is good" (Psalms 73:28). Achieving nearness to *Hashem* is sufficient reason for need for the Tabernacle. The Ramban expressed the following view of the ultimate purpose of the Tabernacle:

"The secret of the Tabernacle is that the Glory which abode upon Mt. Sinai [openly] should abide upon it (the Tabernacle) in a concealed manner." (Exodus 25:1).

Thus, for the Ramban, the concept of, and the need for, a Tabernacle is independent of the need for communal repentance which itself came about as a result of the sin of the Golden Calf. Rather it was to be a portable Mt. Sinai; a means of having G-d dwell continuously in the midst of the Israelite community.

One of the most admirable and inspiring characteristics of the classical Torah commentators is their striving for truth in commentary. Their desire to arrive at a correct understanding of the Torah-text, was unemcumbered and uncontaminated by their own personal ego needs. The classic example comes from Rashi himself in his oft-quoted comment to Genesis 28:5:

וַיִּשְׁלַח יִצְחָק אֶת יַעֲקֹב וַיֵּלֶךְ פַּדֶּנָה אֲרָם אֶל לָבָן בֶּן בְּתוּאֵל הָאֲרַמִּי אֲחִי רִבְקָה אֵם יַעֲקֹב וְעֵשָׂו.

אם יעקב ועשו. איני יודע מה מלמדנו.

The mother of Jacob and Esau: *Rashi*. I don't know what this teaches us.

Certainly Rashi could have passed over the verse with no comment. Instead he chose to point out a redundancy in this verse; he did not hesitate to admit his own inability to explain it. In this way he encouraged the student to pursue the question and possibly come up with an answer of his own.

Actually the tradition of intellectual honesty and personal modesty in teaching Torah began long before Rashi. The Torah recounts (see Leviticus 10 ff.) that on the day of the inauguration of the Tabernacle, two of Aaron's sons, Nadav and Avihu, died in G-d's wrath when they brought a self-initiated offering. The inauguration ceremony required certain sacrificial offerings, some of which were to be eaten by Aaron and his sons. Moses chastised his brother Aaron for not partaking of the sin offering. Aaron then defended himself by explaining that due to his state of mourning, he was exempt. Moses' reaction (Leviticus 10:20) is recorded by the Torah:

וַיִּשְׁמַע מֹשֶׁה וַיִּיטַב בְּעֵינָיו.

וייטב בעיניו. הודה ולא בוש לומר לא שמעתי.

And it was good in his eyes: *Rashi*: He admitted his error and was not ashamed [to do so] saying, [instead of admitting it] "I have not heard this," [instead he said "I heard but forgot."]

WHAT IS RASHI SAYING? _____

In simple terms, Rashi is saying that Moses readily admitted that he had forgotten the law and that Aaron had acted correctly. Moses didn't let personal embarrassment prevent him from admitting his error.

The Ramban illustrates intellectual honesty in another striking way. He disagrees with Rashi in the understanding of a word in Genesis 35:16.

Following is Rashi's comment:

וַיִּסְעוּ מִבֵּית אֵל וַיְהִי עוֹד **כִּבְרַת הָאָרֶץ** לָבוֹא אֶפְרָתָה וַתֵּלֶד רָחֵל וַתְּקַשׁ בְּלִדְתָּהּ.

כברת הארץ: מנחם פירש לשון כביר, רבוי מהלך רב. ואגדה בזמן שהארץ חלולה ומנוקבת ככברה שהניר מצוי הסתיו עבר והשרב עדיין לא בא. ואין זה פשוטו של מקרא שהרי בנעמן מצינו יולך מאתו כברת ארץ'. ואומר אני שהוא שם מדת קרקע כמו מהלך פרסה או יותר כמו שאתה אומר צמד כרם, חלקת שדה, כך במהלך אדם נותן שם מדת קרקע כמו כברת ארץ.

A Kivras of land: Menachem ben Saruk explained the word as having the meaning of כביר (a lot), i.e. a great distance. A *midrashic* explanation is: 'at the time when the ground is full of holes like a sieve, when there was plenty of ploughed ground. The winter passed but the dry season had not yet come.' This, however, cannot be the literal sense of the verse for in the case of Naaman we find 'and he departed from him a כברת of land.' [here meaning that he had walked away but a small distance from Naaman when Gehazi immediately ran after him]. I (Rashi) say this is a measure of land..."

Following is the Ramban's comment on the verse. First he quotes Rashi as above then he writes:

The correct interpretation is that which Rabbi David Kimchi had advanced i.e. that the letter "כ" in the word כברת is the כ of comparison and is not a root letter of the word, the basic word being as in the verses: "They were לברות 'levaros' (food) for them"; ותברני 'Vetavereini (and give me to eat) bread' meaning a small amount of food in the morning. And here the meaning of כברת is the distance walked from the morning to the time of eating, for all travelers measure distance in this manner."

The Ramban then adds the following candid comment:

"This I originally wrote when still in Spain, but now that I was worthy and came to Jerusalem — praise to G-d who is kind and deals kindly! — I saw with my eyes that there is not even a mile between Rachel's grave and Bethlehem. This explanation of Rabbi David Kimchi has thus been refuted... Rather it is a name for a measure of land, as Rashi had said...."

We see clearly how the Ramban, once he had a chance to see with his own eyes the short distance between Rachel's grave and Bethlehem, realized that he had erred and that Rashi's interpretation was correct. (Rashi, himself, never lived in Eretz Yisroel. His interpretation was based on his knowledge of Biblical Hebrew.) The Ramban thought it appropriate to write his own, incorrect, interpretation and then to retract publicly and write the correct interpretation of Rashi. Here, the Ramban has shown us a remarkable example of unadorned intellectual honesty, which is a hallmark of Torah commentators.

Lesson

These teachers of Torah have repeatedly shown us that the search for truth in Torah study requires us to be able to admit our ignorance. Confronting a difficulty in the text for which we have no solution, in no way detracts from the Torah's validity; rather, it reflects on our own limited capacity to fully comprehend everything about the Torah.

With having said this, I would ask the reader to keep in mind the following: The body of this book, the various attempts at analysis of Rashi's and the Ramban's commentary, are *my* attempts to understand them. They are, for the most part, based on the insights of the super-commentaries on Rashi and the Ramban. But the final product as presented in this book, is the result of *my* understanding and, thus, is limited by my limited knowledge. As always in the study of Torah, differences of opinion, counter-arguments and evidence to the contrary are always welcome. They are the breeding ground of new insights and clearer understandings of the "words of the living G-d."

Sources

A word about the sources used in researching this book. The commentaries on Rashi, *Rishonim* and *Acharonim*, devoted their efforts to interpreting what his comment means, what difficulty in the text prompted it and what support there is for it. I have made use of many such supercommentaries. Many Rashi comments were analyzed with the help of more than one commentator. Some were based on my own understanding. Instead I have chosen the path of the author of the famous Tanach commentary *Meztudas Dovid*. He writes the following at the end of his classic commentary:

"Since it was virtually impossible to mention in each place from whose womb what went forth and who begat it, I find myself obligated to list here the names of the commentators from whom I gathered and refined this commentary. This should be considered as if I specified them throughout [my commentary.]"

I too will mention those supercommentaries whose wisdom I made use of.

Almosnino, Shmuel; *Amer Nakeh*,Bartinuro, Ovadia; *Be'er Basadeh*; *Be'er Mayim Chayim*; *Be'er Yitzchak*; *Beurim L'Pirush Rashi,* Lubavitcher Rebbi, Reb Menachim Mendel Schneirson; *Da'as Zekeinim Mi'Balei Hatosaphos*; *Devek Tov*; *Divrei Dovid*; *Divrei Negidim*; *Gur Aryeh* (Maharal); *Havanas HaMikra*; *Heichal Rashi*; Ibn Ezra, Avraham; K'nizel, Yaakov; Leibowitz, Nechama, *Eyunim, Shemos*; *Levush HaOrah*; *LiPhshuto shel Rashi*; *Marashah*; *Maskil L'Dovid*; *Mesiach Illmim*; *Metsudah Chumash/Rashi*; *Minchas Yehudah*, Mizrachi, Eliyahu; *Nachalas Ya'akov*; *Nimukei Shmuel*; *Ohr HaChayim*; *Parshandasah*; *Pentateuch with Rashi* (Rosenbaum & Silbermann); *Perush HaRamban*, Chavel; *Perushei Rashi*, Chavel; *Rashbam*; *Rashi al HaTorah* (Berliner); *Rashi Hashalem* (Ariel); *Rashi on the Torah*, Saperstein Edition (Artscroll); *Sefer Zikaron*; *Sifsei Chachomim*; *Toras Maram*, Reich, Mordecai; *Tzeida Laderech*; *Yosef Hallel*.

A Last Word

For the student who wants to delve deeper on his own, I cite at the end of each analysis those supercommentaries who formed the basis for my analysis of the Rashi comment. It should be understood that the commentaries on Rashi frequently offer different approaches to any one comment. I have used my judgement in choosing those that seem to best explain the comment. But certainly there are other possible interpretations. One of the purposes of this book is to help the student begin using his own analytical skills to decipher Rashi. I would be untrue to this goal if I, myself, did not ultimately rely on my judgement in interpreting Rashi. At the same time, I am fully aware that my judgement is limited. The study of Torah thrives on the interchange of different opinions. It is the give and take that results from various opinions in Torah study that has been called *L'Hagdil Torah U'L'hadirah*, "to make the Torah great and to glorify it." I would be quite happy, actually excited, if the book lead to "conversations" about the best way to understand Rashi.

It is my hope that these books will inspire students to approach the Torah and its commentaries with a disciplined approach, a renewed respect and, what I consider most important, an exhilarating joy of learning.

The centrality of the joy of learning in Torah study is not just a personal preference. Its significance finds expression in our daily prayers. The following words are found in the prayer said before Torah study:

והערב נא ה׳ אלוקינו את דברי תורתך בפינו ובפי עמך ישראל.

"Please, *Hashem*, our G-d, sweeten the words of Your
Torah in our mouth and in the mouths of Your people
Israel."

The words of Torah are sweet when we engage ourselves in their study, when we discuss them with others and when we are inspired to new insights by them. It is my wish that this book be an aid and encouragement in that joyful endeavor.

A complex comment requiring piece by piece analysis.

Exodus 1:10

הָבָה נִתְחַכְּמָה לוֹ פֶּן יִרְבֶּה וְהָיָה כִּי תִקְרֶאנָה מִלְחָמָה וְנוֹסַף גַּם
הוּא עַל שֹׂנְאֵינוּ וְנִלְחַם בָּנוּ וְעָלָה מִן הָאָרֶץ.

וְעָלָה מִן הָאָרֶץ: עַל כָּרְחֵינוּ. וְרַבּוֹתֵינוּ דָּרְשׁוּ כְּאָדָם שֶׁמְּקַלֵּל עַצְמוֹ
וְתוֹלֶה קִלְלָתוֹ בַּאֲחֵרִים, וַהֲרֵי הוּא כְּאִלּוּ כָּתַב יַעֲלֵינוּ מִן הָאָרֶץ —
וְהֵם יִירָשׁוּהָ.

And he will go up out of the land: *Rashi*: Against our will. But our Rabbis explained [that they spoke] like a person cursing himself, but ascribes the curse to others [because he doesn't want to be the object of his own curse]; it is as if it were written 'and *we* shall have to go up out of the land' - and they will take possession of it.

QUESTIONING RASHI

Rashi offers two interpretations in this comment. The first is a *p'shat* interpretation, the second, midrash. Let us look at the first comment. Because it is brief it looks like a Type II Rashi-comment. That is, the comment is *not* meant to answer a difficulty in the verse (i.e., a "What's Bothering Rashi ?" type-comment). Rather it is meant to help us avoid a possible misunderstanding. Our question in such a case is:

What misunderstanding are we to avoid?

YOUR ANSWER:

WHAT MISUNDERSTANDING ARE WE TO AVOID?

An Answer: The verse tells us of the Egyptians' fears. Their fears: Since the Israelites were swiftly increasing in numbers, they might join their enemies and make war with them. If this would happen, we would expect the Egyptians to be glad that the Israelites "will go up from the land" i.e. leave Egypt. Thus we might misunderstand the words "he will go up from the land" to be something they would be happy to see. Rashi's brief comment tells us that this is *not* a desired eventuality. He says that if the Israelites "go up from the land" it would be against the Egyptians' will.

How does Rashi know this? Maybe in fact they would be happy to see them leave.

Hint:

For your answer, look at the whole verse.

YOUR ANSWER:

UNDERSTANDING RASHI

An Answer: Our verse lists a series of developments, which may occur as a consequence of the Israelites' "increase." They are: If there is a war, they will join our enemies, fight us, and go up from the land. We know that *all* of these eventualities were feared, because they all follow the word "lest..." So, "going up from the land" was also feared and if it would happen it would be "against their will."

FURTHER QUESTIONING RASHI

But even though the Torah clearly implies that the Egyptians would not want the Israelites to leave, we should ask: Why wouldn't they want them to leave? After all they were their enemies!

Think! Don't give the first answer that comes to mind, it might be wrong!

YOUR ANSWER:

A POSSIBLE ANSWER...AND ITS REFUTATION

We might say that the Egyptians didn't want their slaves to leave. This was a free work force of 600,000 men! So, maybe this is why the Egyptians saw their leaving as a negative consequence.

This explanation is given by some Rashi commentators. But it can't be correct. Why not?

YOUR ANSWER:

An Answer: If you read verses 9-14, you see that the enslavement of the Israelites came *after* this verse. The decision to enslave them was a *result* of their fears and thus they couldn't have wanted to hold on to
their slaves, because they weren't yet slaves !

So why, then, were the Egyptians distressed by the thought of the Israelites' leaving their country?

YOUR ANSWER:

An Answer: I would suggest that the attitude of the Egyptians towards the Israelites was an ambivalent one. On the one hand, they knew the Jews
contributed much to their economy and they valued their presence.
But at the same time they feared the Jews. Feared they would wax
stronger than their hosts and take charge. This ambivalent attitude
of the host country towards the Jews has been characteristic of the
Jewish experience throughout their history. The Golden era of the
Jews in Spain preceded their expulsion. So too in Germany in the
20th Century, the Jews' contribution to Germany's science, art and
culture was exceptional, nevertheless it was soon followed by the
Holocaust . We also find an explicit example of this in the Torah as
well. Can you find it?

YOUR ANSWER:

An Answer: See Genesis 26:13 ff. There you will find the reaction of Abimelech,
King of the Philistines, to Isaac's monetary success.

"The man [Isaac] became great and kept becoming greater until he
was exceedingly great. ...and the Philistines envied him... And
Abimelech said to Isaac "Go away from us, for you have become
much mightier than we [עצמת ממנו מאד]."

Compare this with our verse. "Behold the people of the Children of Israel are great and mightier than we [עצום ממנו]." See how the Torah uses
similar words to draw our attention to the similar, typical reaction of a
host country to the Jew's success.

So we can assume that Pharaoh and his countrymen both admired and
feared the Israelites' growth. This would lead to an ambivalent attitude
towards them; on the one hand, he would want to enslave them because

of his fear of them, on the other hand, it would not be in their best interests if the Israelites left, i.e., "going up out of the land." He would want to prevent their leaving his country.

This explains Rashi's comment "against their will."

QUESTIONING RASHI'S FIRST INTERPRETATION

Question: Why does he offer a second, *drash*, interpretation?

The fact that Rashi offers another interpretation to the words "he will go up from the land" indicates that he feels his first comment didn't exhaust matters.

What is insufficient with it?

Hint:

This is a subtle point. Read carefully the whole verse. Get the gist of it. What does it say? Who was making war with Egypt? For what purpose?

What's bothering Rashi?

YOUR ANSWER:

A PROBLEM WITH THE FIRST INTERPRETATION

An Answer: The Egyptians feared that the Israelites, by joining these enemies, would leave the country. If so, the phrase "*they* (the Israelites) *may join our enemies*" is misleading. As written, the phrase places the Israelites' goals as subordinate to the enemies, implying that the Israelites would help the enemies of Egypt achieve the latter's goals. The goal of the enemies would probably be to gain domination over Egypt, as is usually the case in aggressive warfare. Their military goals would hardly include freeing the Jews. If our phrase meant to tell us that the war would lead to the Jews leaving Egypt, it should rather have said, "and our enemies *will join them* (the Israelites) and they will go up out of the land."

This is a difficulty with the first interpretation. This may be what is bothering Rashi. He offers the *midrashic* interpretation to overcome this difficulty. How does the second interpretation avoid this difficulty?

YOUR ANSWER:

UNDERSTANDING RASHI'S SECOND INTERPRETATION_____

An Answer: By changing the word "he will go up" which referred to the Israelites, to "we will go up" referring to the Egyptians themselves, Rashi
has surmounted the difficulty. With this interpretation, the normal
concept of warfare is reintroduced: The enemy will conquer the
land and drive the inhabitants out. This is what the Egyptians feared.

A NOTE ON THE PASSOVER HAGGADAH _____

In the Passover Haggadah we read the following *drash* on the verse in
Deuteronomy 26:6. It is appropriate to mention it here since that *drash*
makes reference to our verse:

וַיָּרֵעוּ אֹתָנוּ הַמִּצְרִים וַיְעַנּוּנוּ וַיִּתְּנוּ עָלֵינוּ עֲבֹדָה קָשָׁה.

> וירעו אותנו המצרים כמה שנאמר: הבה נתחכמה לו פן ירבה
> והיה כי תקראנה מלחמה ונוסף גם הוא על שונאינו ונלחם בנו
> ועלה מן הארץ.
>
> **And the Egyptians treated us badly:** as it says: "Come
> let us deal wisely with him lest he increase and it will be
> when there will be a war and he will join our enemies and
> fight us and he will go up from the land."

For those who read the Haggadah every year this is a familiar *drash*. Yet
looked at critically, it is far from easy to understand. Of all possible
verses, why is this verse cited as evidence that the Egyptians treated us
badly? There are certainly more appropriate verses in the beginning of
the Book of Exodus to indicate the Egyptians' cruel treatment to the
Israelites. In fact, this verse itself says nothing of the Egyptians mal-
treating the Israelites. Can you explain this?

Hint:

How does the Haggadah interpret the caption words וירעו אותנו המצרים?

YOUR ANSWER:

An ANALYSIS _____

An Answer: Our sentence, telling of the Egyptians' fear that the Israelite guests
will wage war against them, is used as proof-text and explanation
for the verse in Deuteronomy. The Egyptians suspect the Israelites
of conspiring evil against them. Why?

On the surface, it would seem that the verse in Deuteronomy only tells that the Egyptians were bad to the Israelites.

What is it about the verse that lends itself to this unusual interpretation?

Hint:

Read it carefully.

YOUR ANSWER:

EXPLAINING THE HAGGADAH—A CLOSER LOOK

An Answer: The words ויֵרֵעוּ אוֹתָנוּ are awkward. If the Torah meant to tell us that " they did us evil", it should have said וַיָּרֵעוּ **לָּנוּ** The Torah's words וַיָּרֵעוּ **אוֹתָנוּ** can literally be translated "And they *made us bad*" which could mean "and they attributed badness to us." This grammatical nuance would seem to be the basis for the Haggadah's unusual *drash*. This concept, of attributing evil intentions to the Israelites, is precisely the second interpretation which Rashi offers.

(See Maharshah, Leibowitz, Eyunim)

❖❖❖

Rashi's use of midrash instead of p'shat must be understood.

Exodus 2:2

וַתַּהַר הָאִשָּׁה וַתֵּלֶד בֵּן וַתֵּרֶא אֹתוֹ כִּי טוֹב הוּא וַתִּצְפְּנֵהוּ שְׁלֹשָׁה יְרָחִים.

כִּי טוֹב הוּא: כשנולד נתמלא הבית כלו אורה.

That he was good: *Rashi:* When he was born the whole house was filled with light.

QUESTIONING RASHI

Certainly this isn't the simple *p'shat* of the words "that he was good." Why does Rashi offer this *midrashic* interpretation? Is something about these words bothering him?

Hint:

Read the whole verse.

What might be bothering Rashi?

YOUR ANSWER:

WHAT IS BOTHERING RASHI?

An Answer: If we take the verse at face value, it says in effect: The woman saw that her son was good and therefore she decided to try to save him, by hiding him. The obvious question is: Wouldn't any mother want to save her son? Isn't every child "good" enough to try to save from certain death? Therefore Rashi rejects the "simple meaning."

How does the *midrashic* interpretation answer the question?

YOUR ANSWER:

UNDERSTANDING RASHI

An Answer: A reason had to be found why Moses' mother tried to save him when no other Jewish mother did likewise for her son. By citing the *midrash* that some supernatural sign was evident at Moses' birth—the house was filled with light—she realized that perhaps her efforts to save him would be successful. This, then, is the cause of (and connection with) the following words "and she hid him for three months." She saw that he was good (i.e., the light emanating from him) and therefore decided to hide him.

A common rule for interpreting the words of the Torah according to *p'shat* is that when two facts are brought together in the same sentence they are probably connected in some way, either in a causal or in an associative way. In our sentence the two parts are connected in a causal way: "She saw that he was good (supernatural light)" and therefore "she hid him."

UNDERSTANDING THE MIDRASH

Rashi's comment is based on a *midrash* and is not what we would consider straight *p'shat*. *Midrash* has its own characteristic methods of interpretation. A common one is the *Gezera Shavah* (word association). In our verse we have, "And she saw that he was good (כי טוב)." These same words כי טוב are found elsewhere in the Torah.

Can you think where?

YOUR ANSWER:

Answer: In Genesis 1:4 where it says:

וַיַּרְא אֱלֹקִים אֶת הָאוֹר **כִּי טוֹב** וַיַּבְדֵּל אֱלֹקִים בֵּין הָאוֹר וּבֵין הַחֹשֶׁךְ.

And G-d saw the **light that it was good**; and G-d separated between the light and the darkness.

Here we see that the very same words, כי טוב, that are used to describe
the child Moses, are also used to describe the light at Creation. This
word association is the basis for the *midrashic* interpretation that at
Moses' birth there was a supernatural light in the house.

Exodus 2:13

וַיֵּצֵא בַּיּוֹם הַשֵּׁנִי וְהִנֵּה שְׁנֵי אֲנָשִׁים עִבְרִים נִצִּים וַיֹּאמֶר לָרָשָׁע
לָמָּה תַכֶּה רֵעֶךָ.

> **לָמָּה תַכֶּה:** אַף עַל פִּי שֶׁלֹּא הִכָּהוּ נִקְרָא רָשָׁע בַּהֲרָמַת יָד.
> **Why would you strike:** *Rashi:* Although he had not yet
> smitten him, he is termed "wicked" (רשע), because he had
> merely raised his hand against him.

What would you ask on Rashi's comment?

YOUR QUESTION:

QUESTIONING RASHI

A Question: Rashi says the "wicked one" had *not actually hit* his fellow Jew,
just raised his hand. But the verse seems to say that he did hit him.
On what evidence does Rashi draw his conclusion? Or, in other
words:

What's bothering Rashi here?

Hint:

Look at the Hebrew in the *dibbur hamaschil.*

YOUR ANSWER:

UNDERSTANDING RASHI

An Answer: The word תכה literally means, "You will smite." It is the second person future form of the word להכות. If he had already hit his fellow Jew or was presently hitting him, it should have said למה למה אתה מכה or הכית.

It is this grammatical anomaly that leads Rashi to his *drash* interpretation.

A CLOSER LOOK

Notice Rashi's wording: He says, "he is termed wicked." Why doesn't Rashi say, "Moses called him wicked"?

YOUR ANSWER:

An Answer: Because, in fact, it wasn't Moses who referred to him as wicked, it was the Torah's narration that used the term, "wicked one." This means that the Torah, itself, proclaimed him wicked. Thus raising one's hand against another is a wicked deed according to the Torah.

A FURTHER NOTE

In biblical Hebrew, past, present and future grammatical constructions often do not carry their usual time connotation. We frequently find the future used for the past. For example, אז ישיר משה, "Then will Moses sing..." (Exodus 15:1), when this is actually relating to an event that already occurred. We also find the past tense used for the ongoing present as in נהלת בעזך אל נוה קדשך, "You led with Your might unto Your holy dwelling place" (Exodus 15:13). Here, the past tense is used to describe an event that had yet to take place, i.e., reaching G-d's holy dwelling place (the Land of Israel). So, while the unusual use of time tense is not unusual in the Torah, Rashi will, nevertheless, comment on these anomalies and offer a *drash* interpretation to explain them.

These comments point out the subtle difference between the terms p'shuto *and* mashma'o.

Exodus 2:14

וַיֹּאמֶר מִי שָׂמְךָ לְאִישׁ שַׂר וְשֹׁפֵט עָלֵינוּ הַלְהָרְגֵנִי אַתָּה אֹמֵר כַּאֲשֶׁר הָרַגְתָּ אֶת הַמִּצְרִי וַיִּירָא מֹשֶׁה וַיֹּאמַר אָכֵן נוֹדַע הַדָּבָר.

וַיִּירָא מֹשֶׁה: כפשוטו. ומדרשו, דאג לו על שראה בישראל רשעים דלטורין. אמר, מעתה שמא אינם ראוין להגאל.

אָכֵן נוֹדַע הַדָּבָר: כמשמעו. ומדרשו נודע לי הדבר שהייתי תמה עליו, מה חטאו ישראל מכל שבעים אומות להיות נרדים בעבודת פרך, אבל רואה אני שהם ראויים לכך.

Moses was afraid: *Rashi:* [Understand this] As its Plain Meaning "*k'p'shuto*". But its *midrashic* interpretation is: He was concerned that he saw among the Israelites wicked people who were informers. He thought: If this is so, then perhaps they do not deserve to be redeemed.

So the matter is known: *Rashi:* [Understand this] As its literal meaning "*k'mashma'o*". But its *midrashic* interpretation is: It is known to me that matter about which I was puzzled—how has Israel sinned more than all the seventy nations that they should be subjugated by oppressive labor ? But I now see that they deserve it.

What Is Rashi Saying?

In each of these two Rashi-comments, Rashi offers a *p'shat* interpretation and then a *midrashic* one. The Plain Meaning of these verses deals with the here and now, while the *midrash* attributes to Moses' behavior a timeless, moral implication.

In one case, Rashi calls the first interpretation "*p'shuto*," while in the second comment, he refers to his first interpretation as "*mashma'o*." Why? What is the difference between "*p'shuto*" and "*mashma'o*"?

Can you discern a difference?

Your Answer:

RASHI'S TERMINOLOGY

An Answer: The difference is a subtle, but useful, one. *P'shuto* means the interpretation is based on the contextual meaning; the verse is interpreted according to its context.

Mashma'o, on the other hand, means the word's literal meaning. There is a difference between these two. Sometimes the two coincide, sometimes they don't. We will see two examples to help clarify this.

A good example which illustrates the difference is Rashi's various interpretations of the word יד "hand." Look at Genesis 32:14 where it tells of Jacob preparing a gift for Esau his brother.

וַיָּלֶן שָׁם בַּלַּיְלָה הַהוּא וַיִּקַּח מִן הַבָּא בְיָדוֹ, מִנְחָה לְעֵשָׂו אָחִיו.

> **הבא בידו:** ברשותו . . . ומדרש אגדה, **מן הבא בידו.** –אבנים
> טובות ומרגליות שאדם צר בצרור ונושאם בידו.
>
> **Which came to his hand**: *Rashi*: In his possession, ...
> The *midrashic* explanation of מן הבא בידו is precious stones
> and jewels which a person ties in a packet and carries
> them in his hand.

See how Rashi gives two interpretations of the word יד; one is *midrash*, one is not.

The *p'shat* explanation is "in his possession" which fits in with the context, the plain sense of the verse. But it is not the literal translation of יד. The *midrash* takes the word literally, holding the precious stones in his hand. But no precious stones are mentioned here and it doesn't seem likely that they were lying around. So, in this case, the *mashma'o* (literal) is not *p'shat*.

Another Rashi comment will show us how *p'shuto* and *mashma'o* are similar. In Genesis 24:10 where Abraham's servant sets out to find a bride for Isaac and takes his master's possessions with him.

וַיִּקַּח הָעֶבֶד עֲשָׂרָה גְמַלִּים מִגְּמַלֵּי אֲדֹנָיו וַיֵּלֶךְ וְכָל טוּב אֲדֹנָיו בְּיָדוֹ וְגוֹ'.

> **וכל טוב אדוניו בידו:** שטר מתנה כתב ליצחק על כל אשר לו
> כדי שיקפצו לשלוח לו בתם.
>
> **All the best of his master in his hand**: *Rashi:* He
> [Abraham] wrote a gift-deed to Isaac of all his posses-
> sions so that they would be eager to send their daughter
> to him.

It is inconceivable that the servant could hold *all* of Abraham's possessions literally (*mashma'o*) in his hand. But it is possible and reasonable that he held a document in his hand. So this interpretation of יד is both *p'shuto*, because it makes sense in the context of the verse and it is also *mashma'o*, because it takes יד in the literal, flesh and blood, sense.

With this in mind, we can look again at our verses.

Moses was afraid: *Rashi*: [Understand this] as its Plain Meaning "*k'p'shuto*."

The plain meaning here, based on the context, is clearly that Moses was afraid that his having killed the Egyptian was known and that he would be caught and punished for it. Rashi stressed the *p'shuto* here (the contextual meaning) and not the *mashma'o*, (the literal meaning) since here in both the *drash* and the *p'shat* these words mean literally "Moses was afraid."

Let us now look at the second comment.

So the matter is known: *Rashi*: [Understand this] as its literal meaning "*k'mashma'o*."

The "matter" referred to here is literally Moses' killing the Egyptian. Also "the matter is known" cannot literally mean "It is known to me." If the meaning was that Moses knew something, it should have said simply "I know." So the point Rashi stresses here is the literal meaning of these words—"*mashma'o*."

(See Leibowitz, Eyunim)

A comment which offers a fascinating revelation of Rashi's intent and an ingenious interpretation by the Gaon of Vilna.

Exodus 2:23

וַיְהִי בַיָּמִים הָרַבִּים הָהֵם וַיָּמָת מֶלֶךְ מִצְרַיִם וַיֵּאָנְחוּ בְנֵי יִשְׂרָאֵל מִן הָעֲבֹדָה וַיִּזְעָקוּ וַתַּעַל שַׁוְעָתָם אֶל הָאֱלֹקִים מִן הָעֲבֹדָה.

וימת מלך מצרים: נצטרע והיה שוחט תינוקות ישראל ורוחץ בדמם.

And the king of Egypt died: *Rashi:* he was stricken with leprosy and he slaughtered Israelite babies and bathed in their blood.

This is certainly a comment based on *drash*. What would you ask?

YOUR QUESTION:

QUESTIONING RASHI

Those familiar with this Rashi-comment are accustomed to cite the talmudic statement (*Nedarim* 64b) "Four are considered as dead: the poor, the leper, the blind, and he who has no children." And this is why Rashi says that "The king died" means not that he died but that he became leprous, since leprous = dead. But why search for analogies when there is nothing more dead than dead itself! In other words, we ask: why not take the verse at its face value, that the king really died? Why does Rashi cite a *midrash* when the simple meaning is apparently the most reasonable interpretation?

What's bothering Rashi?

Hint:

Read sentence 2:23 completely.

YOUR ANSWER:

WHAT IS BOTHERING RASHI

An Answer: Our verse says "...and the king died and the Children of Israel moaned, etc." Now, if the king actually died why would the Israelites moan and cry out to G-d? They should have rejoiced.

This is probably what is bothering Rashi, which led him to search for another interpretation other than the simple meaning that the king actually died.

How does his comment deal with this problem?

YOUR ANSWER:

UNDERSTANDING RASHI

The fact that the Israelites moaned after the king's death indicates that their situation became worse after his death. With this in mind, the *midrash*'s explanation that the king didn't actually die, becomes reasonable. He was "symbolically" dead, i.e., leprous. His search for a cure led him to slaughter Israelite infants. His using their blood would explain their outcry.

ANOTHER INTERPRETATION OF RASHI'S COMMENT

The Gaon of Vilna (GRA = Gaon Rabbeinu Eliyahu) offers an ingenious explanation for the *midrash* that Rashi cites. It says in Ecclesiastics 8:8 "There is no dominion on the day of death." This can be interpreted to mean that even when a king dies he has no "dominion," he no longer has any special powers. He is like the rest of mankind, death being the eternal equalizer. And to validate this point he refers us to the first chapters of the Book of Kings. Open up the Tanach and read the first chapter. How is David, King of Israel referred to there? How is he referred to in Chapter 2? Don't be lazy. Look it up! What do you find?

YOUR ANSWER:

Answer: In Chapter 1 when it speaks of David's old age, he is repeatedly referred to as "King David." In Chapter 2, on the other hand it says "And the days of David approached death..." (2:1). No reference is made to "King David" just to "David" he is no longer considered a king, for it is the day of his death. Likewise, whenever a king dies, the Tanach mentions his name without his title "king." The one exception, says the GRA, is King Uziyahu where it does say and "The King Uziyahu died." But there too the Sages say that he didn't really die, rather he was struck with leprosy. So we find a consistency in the *midrashic* interpretation: It almost never says "so-and-so the king died" for "there is no dominion on the day of death." In death." In those rare instances where it does say a king died (Uziyahu and in our case, Pharaoh), the *midrash* explains it not as actual death but as allegorical death—leprosy.

A COMPUTER BASED PROBLEM

This explanation was satisfactory up until the computer CD search was invented! Then someone checked up on the GRA's claim that nowhere else in the Tanach does it say that a "king died" and found, lo and behold, that there is a place where it says a king died.

See chapter 22 in I Kings. There it says "And the king died..." [22:37]. How would the GRA answer this exception?

Read the whole chapter 22. Can you come up with an answer?

YOUR ANSWER:

An Answer: Did you notice how unusual this chapter is? It never refers to the king by his given name! He is always referred to as "the king". So, in such a case there was no choice but to report that "the king died" for no personal name was ever used to identify this king.

The mystery has been solved, the GRA's genius has been reconfirmed and Rashi's *midrash* has been validated. A rule has been discovered which holds up throughout the Tanach. The king was leprous but not actually dead.

(Heard from N. Amsel)

Rashi cites a well known Midrash and the Ramban gives it depth.

Exodus 3:14

וַיֹּאמֶר אֱלֹקִים אֶל מֹשֶׁה אֶהְיֶה אֲשֶׁר אֶהְיֶה וַיֹּאמֶר כֹּה תֹאמַר לִבְנֵי
יִשְׂרָאֵל אֶהְיֶה שְׁלָחַנִי אֲלֵיכֶם.

אהיה אשר אהיה: אהיה עמם בצרה זו אשר אהיה עמם בשעבוד
שאר מלכויות. אמר לפניו, רבונו של עולם, מה אני מזכיר להם
צרה אחרת דיים בצרה זו. אמר לו יפה אמרת כה תאמר וגו'.
I am that I am: *Rashi*. I will be with them in this suffering, I who will be with them in the servitude of other
kingdoms. [Then] Moses said to Him, L-rd of the Universe ! Why should I mention to them other sufferings,
they have enough with this suffering. G-d replied to him:
You have spoken rightly—THUS SHALT THOU SAY
etc. [אהיה has sent me to you] (Without the additional
אשר אהיה).

What question would you ask Rashi about this comment?

YOUR QUESTION:

QUESTIONING RASHI

A Question: Why rely on a *midrash* to explain this verse, it seems clear enough
as it is?

What's bothering Rashi here?

> *Hint:*
>
> Look at the whole verse.

YOUR ANSWER:

WHAT IS BOTHERING RASHI?

An Answer: Actually several things may be bothering Rashi here. First, and
most obvious, is the problem with the two quotes from G-d. First
He tells Moses that His name is אהיה אשר אהיה, then practically in
the same breath, He tells Moses to tell the Israelites that אהיה (alone)
sent him. Why the shortened name?

How does the *midrash* deal with this change in names?

YOUR ANSWER:

Understanding Rashi

An Answer: G-d did shorten the name to be conveyed to the Children of Israel
from אהיה אשר אהיה to אהיה. The *midrash* tells us why He did so.
G-d shortened the name in response to Moses' telling question:
Why should He burden the people with the thought of future suffering when their present predicament was bad enough?

The shortened name of אהיה thus, refers only to the present—G-d will
be with the Children of Israel in their present servitude in Egypt. G-d
accepts Moses' argument and drops all reference to future suffering.

A Closer Look

A closer look at the verse will reveal another problem that was bothering
Rashi.

Do you see a redundancy in it?

Hint:

Reread the verse.

YOUR ANSWER:

What Else Is Bothering Rashi?

An Answer: Twice it says ויאמר "And G-d said to Moses....*and He said*: So
shall you say..." It is G-d speaking both times with no interruption,
why repeat the words, "And He said," twice in the same verse? If it
only had said, "And G-d said," at the beginning of the verse it
would have been sufficient, the same meaning would have been
conveyed.

How does Rashi's comment deal with this redundancy?

YOUR ANSWER:

UNDERSTANDING THE *MIDRASH*

An Answer: The apparently unnecessary repetition implies that something did
in fact transpire between the two "and He said"s. The *midrash* fills
in the missing piece—Moses' retort to G-d, "Why should I mention to them other sufferings, etc." This isn't recorded in the Torah
but the *midrashic* interpretation fills it in.

We see now that that Rashi's comment (based on the *midrash*) explains
both difficulties:

1) The name is in fact shortened, from אהיה אשר אהיה to just אהיה

2) Moses' question to *Hashem* interrupts G-d's words; this is the
reason it says "and He said" twice.

RAMBAN'S INTERPRETATION

The Ramban comments here accepting the *midrash* and expanding on it.

> *Ramban 3:13*
> "This verse calls aloud for an explanation.....[after quot-
> ing Rashi] Thus the language of Rashi quoting the words
> of our Rabbis. Their intent in this Aggadah is as follows:
> Moses had said before Him, blessed be He, 'And they
> shall say unto me: What is His name?,' meaning that G-d
> should tell him the Name which fully teaches His exist-
> ence and His providence. The Holy One, blessed be He,
> answered him: 'Why should they ask for My Name? They
> need no other proof, for I will be with them in all their
> affliction. They shall call, and I will answer.' This is the
> greatest proof that there is a G-d in Israel near us when-
> ever we call upon Him. And verily there is a G-d that
> judges in the earth. This is the correct interpretation of
> the Aggadah."

What does the Ramban mean when he writes "G-d should tell him the Name
which fully teaches His existence and His providence" ? What does he mean by
"existence" and "providence"?

YOUR ANSWER:

Understanding the Ramban

An Answer: By "existence," the Ramban means G-d's essence. The philosophical understanding of the reality of G-d's being. By "providence" he means G-d's guidance and influence in this world.

The Ramban (following the Aggadah) says that G-d's answer is that they have no need of any other proof "for I will be with them in all their affliction."

What does he mean by this? Any other proof of *what*?

Your answer:

An Answer: He is saying there is no need for any other proof of G-d's existence.

How does the quote "for I will be with them ..." explain why they have no need for any other proof ?

Your Answer:

An Answer: The Ramban is making a basic point in Jewish philosophy. The Jew understands the reality of G-d's existence not through philosophical inquiry ("His existence") but by means of G-d's providence, His influence in this world. G-d's protection of the Jewish nation throughout its unique history of exhilarating highs and devastating depths is "proof enough" This is what he means by quoting "for I will be with them in all their afflictions."

We see how the Ramban elaborates on this *Aggadah*, how he gives it philosophical depth. This is an excellent example of a difference between the approaches of the Ramban and Rashi. Rashi will quote a *midrash* without elaboration, leaving the student to accept it as given and interpret it as he will. The Ramban, on the other hand, takes a *midrash* and provides us with explanation of the profound teachings of the Rabbis. Seeing the *midrash* through the Ramban's eyes gives us a glimpse of the wisdom imbedded in the simple looking Aggadah.

The Ramban's Idea and the Kuzari

The idea that G-d's providence and His influence in history are central to Jewish belief, the theme of the Ramban's comment here, can also be seen in Rabbi Judah Hallevi's classic work *The Book of the Kuzari*, which was written a century before the Ramban.

In the dialogue between the King of the Kuzars and the Rabbi, the Rabbi is asked to give the basis of the Jewish belief. We find the following exchange. (Part I).

> "**Rabbi**: I believe in the G-d of Abraham, Isaac and Israel, who led the Children of Israel out of Egypt with signs and miracles; who fed them in the desert and gave them the land, who sent Moses and His law and subsequently thousands of prophets ...
>
> **The King**: Why did you not say that you believe in the Creator of the world, its governor and its guide...?
>
> **Rabbi**: This is based on speculation, conclusions based on thought, but open to many doubts... in the same way did Moses speak to Pharaoh when he said 'The G-d of the Hebrews sent me to you' ... he did not say 'The G-d of heaven and earth sent me to you'..."

Here again, the emphasis is on history, the acts of G-d which are visible and attestable by men and not on the conclusions of philosophical inquiry, which are always open to refutation.

Here we see that p'shat and drash are not synonymous with literal and non-literal.

Exodus 4: 22–23

22. וְאָמַרְתָּ אֶל פַּרְעֹה כֹּה אָמַר ה' בְּנִי בְכֹרִי יִשְׂרָאֵל.

23. וָאֹמַר אֵלֶיךָ שַׁלַּח אֶת בְּנִי וְיַעַבְדֵנִי וַתְּמָאֵן לְשַׁלְּחוֹ הִנֵּה אָנֹכִי הֹרֵג אֶת בִּנְךָ בְּכֹרֶךָ.

> **בני בכורי:** לשון גדולה כמו אף אני בכור אתנהו (תהלים פט:כח)
> זהו פשוטו. ומדרשו כאן חתם הקב"ה על מכירת הבכורה שלקח
> יעקב מעשו.
>
> **My firstborn son**: *Rashi:* [The word "firstborn" here] is an expression of greatness, as (Psalms 89:28) "I will appoint him a firstborn (בכור)". This is the simple meaning *(p'shuto)*. Its *midrashic* comment is: Here the Holy One, blessed be He, set His seal to [confirmed] the sale of the birthright which Jacob had purchased from Esau.

QUESTIONING RASHI

What would you ask on this comment?

YOUR QUESTION:

A Question: Why does Rashi suggest that the simple meaning *(p'shuto)* of בכור is an expression of greatness? Certainly the simple meaning of בכור is not "greatness" but "firstborn."

Do you have an answer?

YOUR ANSWER:

An Answer: In the present context the word בכור refers to all the people of Israel. Certainly they were not all "firstborn."

Another Question:

Remember, whenever Rashi offers two interpretations, we should ask why the need for the second one. Rashi doesn't comment without there being some difficulty in the Torah text nor does he offer a second explanation unless the first is deficient in some way. So here we would ask: Why the need for two interpretations? Why wasn't the *p'shat* sufficient?

What's bothering Rashi?

YOUR ANSWER:

WHAT IS BOTHERING RASHI?

An Answer: Rashi's first interpretation says that we are not to take "firstborn" literally, rather the word means "first in stature." But in the next sentence it says "If you refuse to send him out (G-d's firstborn) then I shall kill your firstborn." There is a "measure for measure" element in this punishment. In fact, eventually, because of the Egyptian refusal to free the Israelites, their firstborn were killed. This would seem to indicate that G-d's words "My firstborn son" are to be taken literally. Perhaps it is for this reason that Rashi searches for another explanation, where "firstborn" is taken literally.

How does the *midrash* help explain the verse?

YOUR ANSWER:

UNDERSTANDING RASHI

An Answer: By telling us that G-d referred to the Israelites as "My firstborn," we see that He considered Esau's sale of the birthright to Jacob (see Genesis 25:29ff) as fully binding. Thus Jacob and his offspring are now actually to be considered G-d's firstborn. Now the punishment is in fact "measure for measure," firstborn for firstborn.

RASHI'S *MIDRASHIC* EXPLANATION

Ironically, Rashi's *midrashic* explanation takes the word "firstborn" literally while his *p'shat* explanation takes the word allegorically. This is a good illustration of the fact that *p'shat* and literal interpretation are not necessarily synonymous.

This is a monumental comment, having great theological and historical import. It all flows directly from the words of the Torah, as Rashi makes clear.

Exodus 6:3

וָאֵרָא אֶל אַבְרָהָם אֶל יִצְחָק וְאֶל יַעֲקֹב בְּאֵל שַׁדָּי וּשְׁמִי הִי לֹא נוֹדַעְתִּי לָהֶם.

וּשְׁמִי הִי **לֹא נוֹדַעְתִּי לָהֶם**. לֹא הוֹדַעְתִּי אֵין כְּתִיב כָּאן אֶלָּא לֹא נוֹדַעְתִּי. לֹא נִכַּרְתִּי לָהֶם בְּמִידַּת אֲמִתּוּת שֶׁלִּי, שֶׁעָלֶיהָ נִקְרָא שְׁמִי הִי נֶאֱמָן לְאַמֵּת דְּבָרַי, שֶׁהֲרֵי הִבְטַחְתִּים וְלֹא קִיַּמְתִּי.

But My name 'Hashem' I was not known to them. *Rashi:* It is not written here לא הודעתי "[My name 'Hashem'] I did not make known [to them]" rather [it says] לא נודעתי "[My name 'Hashem'] I was not known [to them]." I was not recognized by them by My attribute of "keeping faith" by reason of which My name is called 'Hashem,' that I am faithful to substantiate My promises. For indeed I promised them but I have not [yet] fulfilled them.

This is a complex comment; Rashi is addressing two difficulties in our verse. We will begin our analysis by clarifying what he is saying.

WHAT IS RASHI SAYING?

Rashi differentiates between the meaning of two conjugations of the word לדעת "to know." The two are:

1. לא נודעתי, being the passive form, means "I was not known."

2. לא הודעתי, being the active form, means "I did not make known."

Rashi points out that, of these two, our verse says "I was not known."

Now we can question Rashi.

What would you ask here?

YOUR QUESTION:

QUESTIONING RASHI _____

A Question: Why is this grammatical distinction important to point out?

What is bothering Rashi here?

> *Hint:*
>
> Is it true that the name "*Hashem*" (יה-וה) was never used with the Fathers? Can you recall in the book of Genesis the name יה-וה in connection with any of the Fathers?

YOUR ANSWER:

WHAT IS BOTHERING RASHI? _____

An Answer: In fact, G-d did appear to the Fathers using this unique Name. See Genesis 15:7 where it says that G-d appeared to Abraham:

וַיֹּאמֶר אֵלָיו אֲנִי הי אֲשֶׁר הוֹצֵאתִיךָ מֵאוּר כַּשְׂדִּים לָתֶת לְךָ אֶת הָאָרֶץ הַזֹּאת לְרִשְׁתָּהּ.

"And He said to him: I am *Hashem* who brought you out of Ur of the Chaldees to give you this land to possess it."

We also find in Genesis 28:13 in connection with Jacob's ladder dream:

וְהִנֵּה הי נִצָּב עָלָיו וַיֹּאמַר אֲנִי הי אֱלֹקֵי אַבְרָהָם אָבִיךָ וֵאלֹקֵי יִצְחָק הָאָרֶץ אֲשֶׁר אַתָּה שֹׁכֵב עָלֶיהָ לְךָ אֶתְּנֶנָּה וּלְזַרְעֶךָ.

"And behold *Hashem* was standing over him and He said: I am *Hashem*, G-d of Abraham your father and G-d of Isaac; the ground upon which you are lying, to you will I give it and to your descendants."

How then can G-d say here to Moses that He was not known to the Fathers by His unique name? This is what is bothering Rashi.

How does his comment, with its grammatical distinction between נודעתי and הודעתי, help us out of this difficulty?

YOUR ANSWER:

Understanding Rashi

An Answer: If *Hashem* had said "I did not make My name known" (לא הודעתי)
it would have been untrue, since He did tell Abraham and Jacob
this divine name. Rather, what it says here is " I was not known by
My name"(לא נודעתי) this implies the lack of a subjective, personal,
understanding of the significance of this name by Abraham or Jacob.
The meaning is actually that G-d had conveyed His name, but neither Abraham nor Jacob had fully comprehended its meaning. It is
in this sense that the Name was not *known* to them.

This is a subtle point. To understand it, we must understand a basic principle of Torah interpretation with regard to the names of G-d. His names
are not an arbitrary assortment of labels given to the Almighty; instead
each name conveys a particular attribute of G-d. This Rashi stresses when
he says:

לא נכרתי להם **במידת אמיתות שלי**, שעליה נקרא שמי ה',
נאמן לאמת דברי . . .

"I was not recognized by them with *My attribute of "keeping faith"* by reason of which My name is called *Hashem*—
faithful to substantiate My promises..."

The grammatical distinction that Rashi makes is, thus, crucial to a correct understanding of this verse. It correctly avoids the difficulty that
was posed by a superficial reading of the verse.

A Closer Look

Yet there remains another problem in our verse, which Rashi deals with
in a very subtle way. Look at the *dibbur hamaschil* (in Hebrew or English), see if it makes sense. What is wrong here?

YOUR ANSWER:

An Answer: You can say "My name *Hashem,* I did not make known." But once
we use the passive form "I was not known" we cannot say "My
name *Hashem,* I was not known." It doesn't sound right, neither in
Hebrew nor in English. Something is missing in the syntax.

What should it have said?

YOUR ANSWER:

An Answer: It should have said *"with* (or *by)* My Name ...I was not known to them."

How does Rashi deal with this?

> *Hint:*

> Look closely at his every word.

YOUR ANSWER:

An Answer: Rashi, aware of this difficulty, alludes to it in his words " *with* My attribute of keeping faith". See that Rashi adds the letter ב to the words במידת אמיתות . Since "His attribute of keeping faith" is synonymous with the name *Hashem,* it is as if Rashi had written *"with* My name *Hashem* I was not known to them." In this way the difficulty is avoided.

But how does Rashi have the license to do this, to add the word "with"?

> *Hint*:

> Again, look closely at the whole verse.

YOUR ANSWER:

An Answer: Read the whole verse. It says: " I appeared to Abraham, to Isaac and to Jacob *with* the name of *El Shadai* (G-d Almighty), but [*with*] My name *Hashem* I was not known to them." The word "with" appearing earlier in the verse, is carried over to the second part of the verse, thereby elegantly avoiding the syntactical problem.

A DEEPER LOOK

This is truly a monumental Rashi, as we noted at the outset of our analysis. Rashi's comment makes it unequivocally clear that G-d's names in the Torah are not names in the ordinary sense, but are rather terms for His attributes. We must accept this view, otherwise the contradiction between our verse and those in Genesis 15:7 and 28:13 is irreconcilable. This insight shakes the foundation of the school of biblical criticism and its assumption that the names of G-d reflect different scribal traditions and thus, as they claim, the Torah was not written at one time by Moses. For those students unaware of this academic tradition, suffice it to say, that it was this school of thought that contested and helped undermine the Divine authority of the Torah in the eyes of the 'enlightened.' It is referred to as "the Documentary Hypothesis." The Torah view, which vigorously rejects this thesis, is strongly validated by the recognition of the contradiction between our verse and the ones in Genesis. The only way to reconcile this is by means of Rashi's explanation.

(SEE *Mizrachi*)

See how Rashi is concerned with minor, what we might even consider, insignificant, problems in understanding the text.

Exodus 6:4

וְגַם הֲקִמֹתִי אֶת בְּרִיתִי אִתָּם לָתֵת לָהֶם אֶת אֶרֶץ כְּנָעַן אֵת אֶרֶץ מְגֻרֵיהֶם אֲשֶׁר גָּרוּ בָהּ.

וגם הקמותי את בריתי וגו'. וגם כשנראיתי להם באל שדי הצבתי והעמדתי בריתי ביני וביניהם.

I have also established My covenant etc. *Rashi:* And also when I appeared to them as *El Shaddai* I established and set up My covenant between Myself and them.

What can you ask here?

YOUR QUESTION:

QUESTIONING RASHI

A Question: What is Rashi doing here? He seems to be saying what the Torah itself already said. Why belabor the obvious?

What is bothering him?

YOUR ANSWER:

WHAT IS BOTHERING RASHI?

An Answer: The word וגם " also" is problematic here. "Also" usually connects two positive or two negative statements. For example one could say "I went to the store and bought bread and *also* bought milk." But one wouldn't say " I went to the store and bought bread and *also* didn't buy any milk. " Likewise, our verse follows the previous verse where it says negatively "And by My name, *Hashem,* I was not known to them." To continue with the positive statement "and *also* I established etc." doesn't make sense. This is bothering Rashi.

How does Rashi's comment deal with this problem?

YOUR ANSWER:

UNDERSTANDING RASHI

An Answer: Rashi's comment connects the positive statement in our verse ["I established My covenant..."] with the positive statement at the *beginning* of the previous verse, "And I appeared to Abraham ... as El Shaddai," skipping over the latter part of the verse and its negative connotation. We see now the significance of Rashi's first words here, "When I appeared unto them ..."

A CLOSER LOOK

Notice some other slight change Rashi makes here. He substitutes other words for one of the words in the Torah. Which words?

YOUR ANSWER:

Answer: The Torah uses the word והקימותי, Rashi uses two other words הצבתי והעמדתי. Why? This is a bit more difficult.

Hint:

See Genesis 26:3.

YOUR ANSWER:

An Answer: In Genesis 26:3, when G-d speaks with Isaac, He says:

גּוּר בָּאָרֶץ הַזֹּאת וְאֶהְיֶה עִמְּךָ וַאֲבָרְכֶךָּ כִּי לְךָ וּלְזַרְעֲךָ אֶתֵּן אֶת כָּל הָאֲרָצֹת הָאֵל וַהֲקִמֹתִי אֶת הַשְּׁבֻעָה אֲשֶׁר נִשְׁבַּעְתִּי לְאַבְרָהָם אָבִיךָ.

"Dwell in this land and I will be with you and will bless you; for to you and to your offspring will I give all these countries and *I will fulfill* My oath which I swore to Abraham your father."

Here, in this context, the same word והקימותי means "I will fulfill" whereas in our verse it can't mean "fulfill", because the verb is in the past tense and G-d had not yet fulfilled His promise. Therefore in place of "I fulfilled" Rashi substitutes the words "I set up" "I established." He is thus telling us that this word can have other meanings besides "I fulfilled," and thereby avoids a possible misunderstanding.

A Lesson

The above analysis shows how we must understand the purpose of each word in Rashi's comments in order to derive maximum benefit from his precisely worded commentary.

(SEE Mizrachi, Liphshuto shel Rashi)

A simple comment, yet a little reflection reveals some problems in comprehension.

Exodus 7:4

וְלֹא יִשְׁמַע אֲלֵכֶם פַּרְעֹה וְנָתַתִּי אֶת יָדִי בְּמִצְרָיִם וְהוֹצֵאתִי אֶת צִבְאֹתַי אֶת עַמִּי בְנֵי יִשְׂרָאֵל מֵאֶרֶץ מִצְרַיִם בִּשְׁפָטִים גְּדֹלִים.

אֶת יָדִי: יד ממש, להכות בהם.

My hand: *Rashi*: Literally "hand", to smite them.

Whenever Rashi comments on a common word, one that appeared previously in the Torah, we should always ask a question. What question?

YOUR QUESTION:

Questioning Rashi

A Question: Why did Rashi wait until now to make his comment? The word יד "hand", as G-d's hand, was used earlier, see above Exodus 3:20 where it says "And I will stretch out My hand and smite the Egyptians etc." If Rashi saw the need to comment on this term in the context of G-d's hand, why didn't Rashi comment then?

What is bothering Rashi here that leads him to comment?

YOUR ANSWER:

WHAT IS BOTHERING RASHI?

An Answer: Previously when the Torah used the term "hand of G-d" it says explicitly that G-d will smite the enemy. (As in Exodus 3:20. Other examples are Exodus 9:3; 9:15; Deut. 2:15) But in our verse there is no reference to smiting. Rashi therefore finds it necessary to clarify the point and tells us that reference to G-d's hand here means to smite the enemy.

This Rashi-comment looks like a Type II comment, that is, a brief comment intended to steer us away from a misunderstanding. What misunderstanding? Look again at this Torah verse and think how you might have understood the words ונתתי את ידי "and I will put (literally "give") My hand", without Rashi's comment.

YOUR ANSWER:

A POSSIBLE MISUNDERSTANDING

An Answer: The Torah says literally "And I will put My hand in Egypt and I will take out My legions ...from Egypt..." This could very likely be interpreted to mean: G-d will put His hand in the land of Egypt and (with His hand) take out the Israelites from that land. Note the following idiosyncrasies here:
* There is no reference to punishing in this verse.
* The use of the term "*give* My hand" has a positive implication, "giving" is generally a positive concept.
* The phrase "My hand" is immediately followed by the words "I will take out My legions (people) from the Land of Egypt."

All of the above could lead us to think—wrongly—that G-d's hand here is not meant to punish the Egyptians, but rather to help the Children of Israel out of the land of Egypt.

Thus, Rashi tells us otherwise. How does he?

YOUR ANSWER:

UNDERSTANDING RASHI

Rashi says that יד means smiting, not "lifting out" or "extricating". The verse then means that G-d will *smite* the Egyptians (synonymous with "Egypt") with His hand and *then* will He take the Israelites out of the land of Egypt.

ANOTHER QUESTION ON RASHI _____

Can you ask another, rather obvious, question on Rashi's words "hand, literally"?

YOUR QUESTION:

A Question: What does Rashi mean by "hand, literally"? Does G-d have a hand, literally? A hand of flesh and blood? Of course not. One of the most basic concepts in Judaism is the belief that G-d is not corporeal. This anti-anthropomorphic stance is central to the Torah's teachings and is, among other things, what sets it apart from Christianity. G-d has no body and can in no way be conceived of as a physical being. So what could "hand, literally" mean? This question has puzzled many students of Rashi.

YOUR ANSWER:

A DEEPER UNDERSTANDING OF RASHI _____

To understand Rashi's meaning of יד ממש "hand, literally" we have to compare this comment with another Rashi comment where he uses this same term. We find another Rashi-comment on Exodus 14:31. Following is the Torah verse and his comment on it.

וַיַּרְא יִשְׂרָאֵל אֶת הַיָּד הַגְּדֹלָה אֲשֶׁר עָשָׂה הי בְּמִצְרַיִם וגו׳
And Israel saw the great hand which G-d had wielded against Egypt etc.

אֶת הַיָּד הַגְּדֹלָה. אֶת הַגְּבוּרָה הַגְּדוֹלָה שֶׁעָשְׂתָה יָדוֹ שֶׁל הַקָּבָּ״ה,
וְהַרְבֵּה לְשׁוֹנוֹת נוֹפְלִין עַל לְשׁוֹן יָד וְכוּלָן לְשׁוֹן יָד מַמָּשׁ הֵן,
וְהַמְפוֹרְשׁוֹ יְתַקֵּן הַלָּשׁוֹן אַחַר עִנְיַן הַדִּבּוּר.

The great hand. *Rashi:* The great power which the hand of the Holy One Blessed be He had exercised. There are many meanings that are appropriate to the expression יד "hand" but all of them are expressions of hand literally, and he who is explaining it must adapt the language according to the meaning of the passage.

Note that Rashi translates יד here as "power", yet in the same breath he says, "all are expressions of 'hand' literally." This appears to be an outright contradiction. To deepen the confusion he says the word יד must be translated differently according to the context in which it is found. Now either יד means 'hand' literally or it doesn't. According to Rashi יד here means "power," but we know it can also mean "possession." As in Genesis 32:13:

וַיָּלֶן שָׁם בַּלַּיְלָה הַהוּא וַיִּקַּח מִן הַבָּא בְיָדוֹ מִנְחָה לְעֵשָׂו אָחִיו.

And Rashi says there:

מִן הַבָּא בְיָדוֹ: בִּרְשׁוּתוֹ.

From that which had come in his hand: *Rashi*: In his possession.

So we see, as Rashi tells us, that the meaning of this word changes depending on the context.

If so, why does Rashi say "hand, literally" and what could he possibly mean by this? This is a very difficult question.

The *Mizrachi*, the famous super-commentary on Rashi, offers a brief but strange comment here. He says "The Torah speaks in the language of man." This is a Talmudic concept. But this usually means that the use of anthropomorphisms in the Torah are *not* to be taken literally. Yet Rashi here says we are to take the word "hand" literally. Thus it is hard to see how the *Mizrachi's* comment explains away the difficulty with Rashi's comment.

Can you supply an answer?

YOUR ANSWER:

UNDERSTANDING RASHI

As a general rule, in attempting to understand Rashi's commentary, it is important to remember that we are interested in understanding what *Rashi* meant. By that I mean, it is not uncommon in scholarly work to search for answers to questions that make sense to *us*. Sometimes a suggested answer is the product of a brilliant analysis, but in spite of the intellectual fireworks, it may not be Rashi's own intent. To be true to our search for understanding Rashi, we must search for *Rashi's* intent. We can be confident that if we can discover *his* meaning it will be eminently reasonable.

But how can we possibly know what Rashi had in mind? Unfortunately we can't ask him. One way to determine what Rashi meant when he uses a puzzling phrase is to see if he ever uses the same phrase elsewhere in his commentary. Comparing the various uses can shed light on his meaning in our particular verse.

COMPUTER ASSISTED RASHI ANALYSIS

Today, with modern computer technology and the encyclopedic information stored on CD's, with a push of a button we can gain access to information that only the phenomenal memory of Talmudic scholars of previous generations could supply.

An Explanation

A search reveals the following interesting and illuminating source in Tractate *Menachos* 37b.

There the Talmud discusses the question of where the Tefillin of the hand and of the head should be placed. The verse in the Torah (Deut. 6:8) reads:

וּקְשַׁרְתָּם לְאוֹת עַל יָדֶךָ וְהָיוּ לְטֹטָפֹת בֵּין עֵינֶיךָ.

The Talmud rejects the literal meaning of "between your eyes" and says this really means on the front part of the top of the head. It also rejects the literal meaning of "on your hand." The Talmud tells us that יד doesn't mean ידך ממש [note the similarity to Rashi's words] rather it means "on the high part (biceps) of the arm." On the words ידך ממש Rashi makes a revealing one-word comment:

ידך ממש: כף
"your hand, literally: *Rashi*: palm (not arm.)"

We now can grasp what Rashi means in our verse. The word יד can mean either "hand" or "arm." "Hand, literally" means simply the palm of the hand and not the whole arm. That is what Rashi is telling us here. There is nothing philosophical or particularly deep in his choice of the words יד ממש. All he is telling us is that the word here means "palm of the hand" and not the arm.

Why do you think it necessary for Rashi to tell us this?

Hint:

See the complete comment.

Your Answer:

An Answer: Rashi's point is to tell us that the hand of G-d here is for smiting the Egyptians. The palm (fist) is used to hit someone, not the arm.

This too helps us understand Rashi's comment in Exodus 14:31 where he says "all of them are expressions of hand literally." He means all the different uses of the word יד are to be understood as "palm." One holds something in his palm which is in his possession and one uses his fist (closed palm) for hitting and as evidence of one's power.

In summary: Rashi's very brief comment teaches us two things

1. That G-d's hand here was a punishing hand and not a saving hand.
2. That hand here is the palm or fist and not as in another place in the Torah where it means arm.

(See *LiPhshuto shel Rashi*)

Rashi & Ramban argue over language style.

Exodus 8:5

וַיֹּאמֶר מֹשֶׁה לְפַרְעֹה הִתְפָּאֵר עָלַי לְמָתַי אַעְתִּיר לְךָ וְלַעֲבָדֶיךָ וּלְעַמְּךָ לְהַכְרִית הַצְפַרְדְּעִים מִמְּךָ וּמִבָּתֶּיךָ רַק בַּיְאֹר תִּשָּׁאַרְנָה.

לְמָתַי אַעְתִּיר לָךְ. את אשר אעתיר לך היום על הכרתת הצפרדעים, למתי תרצה שיכרתו, ותראה אם אשלים דברי למועד שתקבע לי. אלו נאמר "מתי" אעתיר היה משמע מתי אתפלל, עכשיו שנאמר "למתי" משמע אני היום אתפלל עליך שיכרתו הצפרדעים לזמן שתקבע עלי, אמור לאיזה יום תרצה שיכרתו.

For when shall I pray for you? *Rashi:* With reference to the prayer which I shall make today to destroy the frogs, when do want them to be destroyed, and you will see whether I can carry out my promise by the time that you set for me. If the text had read מתי אעתיר (without the ל), it would mean "when shall I pray?" but now that it says למתי אעתיר it means, I will pray *today* that the frogs be destroyed by the time you set for me. Tell me, then, by what day you wish them destroyed?

WHAT IS RASHI SAYING?

Rashi is quite clear here as to the point of his comment. He wants to clarify the meaning of the word למתי. Since the addition of the ל is unusual, Rashi shows us its special meaning here, Moses will pray now to have the frogs destroyed at whatever time in the future that Pharaoh designates.

RAMBAN'S ARGUMENT AGAINST RASHI

After quoting Rashi's comment here the Ramban says:

'The *p'shat* interpretation is that at the time he prayed, the frogs were removed because it says (8:8) 'and Moses cried out to *Hashem* regarding the frogs which He had brought on Pharaoh. And *Hashem* did according to the word of Moses and the frogs died, etc.' and it does not say 'And *Hashem* did *on the morrow*, etc.' Also the term למתי is no proof that he prayed immediately [for a future removal of the frogs], because the word means the same as מתי, and there are many cases of the additional ל as in (Exodus 8:19) למחר יהיה האות הזה 'tomorrow will be this sign,' or (Deut. 9:7) למן היום אשר יצאת מארץ מצרים 'from the day you went out of Egypt' and many other examples like these."

WHAT IS THE RAMBAN SAYING?

The Ramban makes his point as clearly and emphatically as Rashi makes his. The Ramban is not impressed by the additional ל, he implies it is merely a literary style which the Torah makes use of many times with no difference in meaning from the word מתי without the ל. He supports his case by reference to sentence 8:8 where it says that Moses prays for their removal immediately upon leaving Pharaoh's presence and that *Hashem* removes them, apparently immediately, since there is no mention of the morrow.

Can you describe, in a few words, the difference in approaches of these Torah commentators, their approach to this verse being an example of this?

YOUR ANSWER:

THE DIFFERENCE IN APPROACHES BETWEEN RASHI AND THE RAMBAN

An Answer: It would seem that Rashi is more literal in his interpretation of slight nuances in the Torah's language; the Ramban, more liberal. We see a similar debate on the first verse in *parashas Lech Lecha* (Genesis 12:1). The Ramban refers to the rules of language there. Here too he sees the Torah's language as being more flexible. He seems to say that the Torah has its literary style and slight linguistic nuances do not necessarily imply nuances in meaning. Rashi's approach is more demanding of these nuances, he seems to say that they are not for naught, they must carry some particular meaning.

[But see dispute Rashi-Ramban, Exodus 14:28, where positions are reversed!]

Can you find support for Rashi's interpretation of this verse elsewhere in the text?

Hint:

Look further regarding other plagues.

YOUR EVIDENCE:

SUPPORT FOR RASHI

Rabbeinu Bachaya, in his commentary on the Torah, finds support for Rashi in Exodus 8:25. There, referring to the plague of mixed wild beasts, it says

וַיֹּאמֶר מֹשֶׁה הִנֵּה אָנֹכִי יוֹצֵא מֵעִמָּךְ וְהַעְתַּרְתִּי אֶל הי וְסָר הֶעָרֹב
מִפַּרְעֹה מֵעֲבָדָיו וּמֵעַמּוֹ מָחָר וגו׳

"And Moses said: Behold I leave you and I shall entreat *Hashem* and the mixture of wild beasts will depart from Pharaoh, from his servants and from his people *tomorrow*, etc."

Here it does not say "I shall entreat *Hashem* tomorrow" even though the wild beasts were to be removed only on the morrow. This, says Rabbeinu Bachaya, indicates that Moses would pray immediately for the cessation of a plague to take effect on the morrow.

A CLOSER LOOK AT A PATTERN IN THE PLAGUES

Rabbeinu Bachaya points out an interesting pattern, not usually noticed, in the plagues.

Why would Pharaoh ask for the plagues' cessation on the *next* day, when immediate relief would seem to be the desired objective? Commentaries suggest that Pharaoh was skeptical of Moses and the miraculous nature of the plagues. He assumed that Moses had some insight into natural events and thus predicted these "miracles" which he knew would happen naturally in any event. Thus Pharaoh thought that since Moses asked him when he wanted the plague stopped, Moses expected Pharaoh to say "right now" and Moses was ready for that, because he knew it would stop soon due to natural causes. So Pharaoh thought to outsmart Moses and made the unusual request to stop the frogs only on the morrow, even though this would cause him and his people additional discomfort.

With this in mind, notice the pattern that Rabbeinu Bachaya points out.

See Exodus 8:19 regarding the plague of mixed animals:

וְשַׂמְתִּי פְדֻת בֵּין עַמִּי וּבֵין עַמֶּךָ, לְמָחָר יִהְיֶה הָאֹת הַזֶּה.

And I will put a separation between my people and your people, **tomorrow** will be this sign.

See Exodus 9:5 regarding the plague of pestilence:

וַיָּשֶׂם הי מוֹעֵד לֵאמֹר, מָחָר יַעֲשֶׂה הי הַדָּבָר הַזֶּה בָּאָרֶץ.

And *Hashem* set an appointed time saying: **Tomorrow** *Hashem* will do this thing in the land.

See Exodus 9:18 regarding the plague of hail:

הִנְנִי מַמְטִיר כָּעֵת מָחָר בָּרָד כָּבֵד מְאֹד וגו'

Behold I will rain at this time **tomorrow** very heavy hail, etc.

See Exodus 10:4 regarding the plagues of locusts:

כִּי אִם מָאֵן אַתָּה לְשַׁלֵּחַ אֶת עַמִּי הִנְנִי מֵבִיא מָחָר אַרְבֶּה בִּגְבֻלֶךָ.

For if you refuse to let My people go, behold, **tomorrow** I will bring the locusts in all your boundaries.

PHARAOH'S COMEUPPANCE

It is as if Moses is mocking Pharaoh "You asked me to remove the frogs 'tomorrow' to test me and my G-d, well, then, you will have your tomorrow and tomorrow and tomorrows! You'll wait expectantly for each plague, until... tomorrow.

Rashi & the Malbim argue over p'shat *where contextual clues play a factor.*

Exodus 8:14

וַיַּעֲשׂוּ כֵן הַחַרְטֻמִּים בְּלָטֵיהֶם לְהוֹצִיא אֶת הַכִּנִּים וְלֹא יָכֹלוּ וַתְּהִי הַכִּנָּם בָּאָדָם וּבַבְּהֵמָה.

לְהוֹצִיא אֶת הַכִּנִים. לבראותם [להוציאם] ממקום אחר.
To take out the lice: *Rashi*. To create them [to take them out] from another place.

What is your question on this short and fairly obvious comment?

YOUR QUESTION:

QUESTIONING RASHI

A Question: Isn't what Rashi says obvious ? Isn't this the plain meaning of the verse? Why does he need to comment at all?

What's bothering Rashi?

> Note: This comment has a Type II style, it is very brief. This would mean that the comment is not prompted by a question regarding the text, rather by Rashi's desire to help us avoid a misunderstanding.

What misunderstanding?

YOUR ANSWER:

A POSSIBLE MISUNDERSTANDING

An Answer: The simplest translation of the word להוציא is "to take out" meaning to remove.

> By translating this word as "to create" i.e., to make more lice, Rashi tells us that that it does not mean "to remove."

> But this is quite strange. Why would the scorcerers want to add discomfort to the Egyptians? Haven't they got enough problems as it is? Being that Rashi's interpretation is unusual, we should ask:

> How does Rashi know that this is the correct meaning of the word here?

YOUR ANSWER:

UNDERSTANDING RASHI

An Answer: If we compare the Egyptian magician's reaction to the previous plagues, we see that in each case they tried to imitate Moses' trick, in order to show its insignificance. Their purpose was to show that Israel's G-d is not really particularly powerful, for we too, say the Egyptians, can do whatever your G-d can do. Thus Rashi considers the story as a whole, and views this word as following the pattern already set down in the previous narrative.

SUPPORT FOR RASHI _____

Look for support for Rashi in the words of this verse itself.

YOUR ANSWER:

An Answer: The verse begins with "And they did likewise..." Likewise would mean they too tried to do what Moses had done, i.e., create more lice.

FURTHER SUPPORT FOR RASHI _____

The Hebrew word להוציא is used elsewhere in Tanach to mean "to create". Can you think of where?

Hint:

It is used in a well-known phrase.

YOUR ANSWER:

An Answer: See Psalms 104:14.

מַצְמִיחַ חָצִיר לַבְּהֵמָה וְעֵשֶׂב לַעֲבֹדַת הָאָדָם **לְהוֹצִיא** לֶחֶם מִן הָאָרֶץ.

He causes vegetation to sprout for the animal and plants through man's labor, *to bring forth bread* from the earth.

COMPARE WITH MALBIM _____

The Malbim offers a different interpretation of this phrase.

"According to the Sages, they wanted to make [more lice] but couldn't. But the correct view [of *p'shat*] is that the magicians wanted to *remove them* from the people and the animals. For they already saw that Pharaoh paid no attention to their success in bringing up the frogs (see Ch.8:3). So he [Pharaoh] made the main test of Moses' power to see if the frogs could be removed. Now they [the magicians] wanted to remove the lice."

We see that Malbim offers what we suggested, before we saw Rashi's interpretation.

Notice that the Malbim emphasizes that the test for the magicians switched from duplicating Moses' plague ["Pharaoh paid no attention to their succeeding in bringing up frogs"] to a test of removing the plague.

In this way the Malbim attempts to nullify the assumption behind Rashi's interpretation.

Can you defend the Malbim?

Hint:

Look at this verse carefully, listen to its emphasis.

YOUR ANSWER:

SUPPORT FOR THE MALBIM

An Answer: The verse says:

"The sorcerers did likewise with their incantations להוציא the lice, but they could not. And the lice were on man and animal."

The verse says "they could not. And the lice were on man and animal." The flow of the verse is smooth if להוציא means to remove; we see their failure expressed in the words "and the lice were on man and animal." But if להוציא means "to create" the fact that the lice were on man, etc., in no way reflects the sorcerers failure. Quite the contrary, it makes it sound like they succeeded.

A LESSON

The Malbim lived some 700 years after Rashi, and as every Torah scholar since Rashi's time, he certainly had unreserved admiration for Rashi's genius. Nevertheless he saw fit to disagree with Rashi's interpretation here. The Torah commentator strives for truth; clearly his respect for Rashi was tempered by his desire to discover the truest understanding of the Torah's words. And thus we see the Ramban's great admiration for Rashi, yet, at the same time, if he feels that Rashi's interpretation was not correct, he will dispute his words with vociferous vigor. This thirst for understanding of the Torah finds expression in the Sages' succinct saying (Tractate *Berachos* 62b):

תורה היא וללמוד אני צריך.

It is Torah, and learn it, I must!

A brief comment that requires analysis.

Exodus 10:1

וַיֹּאמֶר הי אֶל מֹשֶׁה בֹּא אֶל פַּרְעֹה כִּי אֲנִי הִכְבַּדְתִּי אֶת לִבּוֹ וְאֶת לֵב
עֲבָדָיו לְמַעַן שִׁתִי אֹתֹתַי אֵלֶּה בְּקִרְבּוֹ.

ויאמר הי אל משה בא אל פרעה. והתרה בו.
And G-d said to Moses: Come to Pharaoh: *Rashi*: And
warn him.

Have you a question on this comment?

YOUR QUESTION:

QUESTIONING RASHI

A Question: Rashi seems to tell us the obvious. Why the need to comment?

   Hint:

   Reread the whole verse.

YOUR ANSWER:

WHAT IS BOTHERING RASHI?

An Answer: Nowhere in the verse does it say why G-d commanded Moses to
come to Pharaoh. The other plagues are usually introduced by "Go
to Pharaoh and say to him" (see Exodus 7:16–17; 7:26); here, no
such command is recorded.

   Furthermore the verse does give a reason for something, for it says
   "*because* I have hardened Pharaoh's heart..." We can ask: What is
   "because"? Certainly it doesn't mean "Go to Pharaoh *because* I

have hardened his heart" ! That's hardly a reason for going to him. Yet that is what the verse seems to say. So the meaning of "because" is not at all clear.

These issues may be what is bothering Rashi.

How does his short comment settle the matter?

YOUR ANSWER:

UNDERSTANDING RASHI

An Answer: By adding the words "to warn him", Rashi answers both questions in one fell swoop. The purpose of Moses' visit is explained ("to warn Pharaoh"). We can now better understand the use of "because" in the verse. G-d tells Moses to come to Pharaoh to warn him of the next plague. Moses may have wondered: Since Pharaoh has already suffered two plagues which made no impression on him, he had been totally unresponsive, what is the point of going once more? The verse therefore continues, as if to answer Moses' question: G-d says: Pharaoh has been unresponsive "because I have hardened his heart" and in spite of that I tell you to go to him and warn him of a future plague.

What evidence can you find that this, in fact, was the point of Moses' visit?

YOUR ANSWER:

SUPPORT FOR RASHI'S INTERPRETATION

An Answer: A few verses further, in 10:4, we read that Moses says to Pharaoh:

"For if you refuse to send forth My people, behold tomorrow I shall bring locusts into your border."

This is the warning that Rashi mentioned in this comment.

(See *Ohr Hachayim*)

A simple, somewhat cryptic, comment that requires understanding.

Exodus 10:11

לֹא כֵן לְכוּ נָא הַגְּבָרִים וְעִבְדוּ אֶת ה׳ כִּי אֹתָהּ אַתֶּם מְבַקְשִׁים וַיְגָרֶשׁ
אֹתָם מֵאֵת פְּנֵי פַרְעֹה.

> **וַיְגָרֶשׁ אֹתָם.** הרי זה לשון קצר, ולא פירש מי המגרש.
> **And he drove them away.** *Rashi:* This is an abbreviated verse; it does not specify who expelled [them].

What Is Rashi Saying?

Rashi notes that something is missing in this verse; nowhere does it tell us who expelled Moses and Aaron from before Pharaoh.

What would you ask here?

Your Question:

Questioning Rashi

A Question: Since Pharaoh is the only one referred to in the previous verses, it would seem obvious that it was Pharaoh who expelled them, even though it doesn't say so explicitly. Why isn't that clear to Rashi?

What's bothering him?

> *Hint:*

Look closely at all the words in this verse.

Your Answer:

What Is Bothering Rashi?

An Answer: The words "And he expelled them *from before Pharaoh*" indicate that it wasn't Pharaoh himself who threw them out, for if it was, it should have stated "And he expelled them *from before him.*" This indicated to Rashi that someone else, unnamed, was involved here.

How does his comment deal with this?

UNDERSTANDING RASHI

Rashi makes us aware that something is missing in this sentence. He doesn't tell us who it was that expelled Moses and Aaron, for there is no way to know that. His basic point is to teach us a rule of the Torah's style, i.e., sometimes we will find a verse which is incomplete. These are termed by him, לשון קצר or מקרא קצר. When Rashi uses these terms he means that we have to fill in the missing words on the basis of compositional logic. The Torah hasn't forgotten them, it has omitted them probably because they are insignificant and, therefore, not necessary to note.

Checking Rashi's midrashic source clarifies an apparent difficulty.

Exodus 11:2

דַּבֶּר נָא בְּאָזְנֵי הָעָם וְיִשְׁאֲלוּ אִישׁ מֵאֵת רֵעֵהוּ וְאִשָּׁה מֵאֵת רְעוּתָהּ כְּלֵי כֶסֶף וּכְלֵי זָהָב.

דבר נא. אין נא אלא לשון בקשה. בבקשה ממך הזהירם על כך, שלא יאמר אותו צדיק אברהם "ועבדום וענו אותם" קיים בהם, "ואחרי כן יצאו ברכוש גדול" לא קיים בהם.

Please speak. *Rashi:* The word נא can only mean [here] 'please.' I beseech you [Moses], please instruct them about this (i.e., that the Israelites should take the silver and gold vessels of the Egyptians), so that the righteous man, Abraham, should not say "He fulfilled [the promise] 'and they will enslave and afflict them' but [the promise] 'and afterwards they will go free with great wealth' He did not fulfill.

WHAT IS RASHI SAYING?

Let us begin this analysis by first understanding what Rashi is saying. First, he says that the word נא in our verse means "please." He certainly doesn't mean that this is what the word *always* means. We know that the word נא can also mean "now" as when Avram speaks with Sarai his wife and says הנה נא ידעתי כי אשה יפת מראה את " Behold, I **now** know that you are a beautiful woman." (Genesis 12:11) The word can also mean "uncooked" as in אל תוכלו ממנו נא "Don't eat from [the Pascal offering]

uncooked." (Exodus 12:9). So Rashi is telling us that in *this* verse the word means "please."

He then explains why G-d was beseeching ("please") Moses to tell the Israelites to take the silver and golden vessels from the Egyptians. The reason: So that Abraham won't have a complaint against G-d.

Now, we're ready for your questions on this Rashi-comment.

What would you ask here?

YOUR QUESTION:

QUESTIONING RASHI

A Question: Why does Rashi offer this remote *drash*? (Taken from the Talmud *Berachos* 9a). What is wrong with the simple meaning of the verse, i.e., G-d is asking Moses to tell the Israelites to take the silver and gold from their Egyptian masters before they depart Egypt ?

Hint:

Are the words in the *dibbur hamaschil* appropriate in our context?

YOUR ANSWER:

WHAT IS BOTHERING RASHI?

An Answer: G-d is pleading ("please") with Moses to tell the people to take "reparations" from the Egyptians, their valuables. The problem is, why the need to say 'please', as if G-d were asking them to do *Him* a favor? Taking the precious vessels should be all too readily appreciated by Moses and by the freed slaves. The poetic justice of despoiling the Egyptians after the all the years that the Egyptians had despoiled them—physically, monetarily and morally—the Israelites would certainly have been ready to fulfill this *mitzvah* without any prompting. Why then the need for the term נא "please" ?

How does Rashi's *drash* deal with this problem?

YOUR ANSWER:

Understanding Rashi

An Answer: Rashi tells us that this was a special request from G-d, Who wanted the freed slaves to take the gold and silver so that Abraham would not accuse Him of not keeping His word completely.

Does that make sense to you? It shouldn't! What would you ask on this *midrash* which Rashi quotes?

Your Question:

Questioning the *Drash*

A Question: If G-d promised Abraham that his offspring would leave Egypt with great wealth, why is G-d concerned that his promise be fulfilled only "so that the righteous man, Abraham, won't complain"? If G-d promised Abraham, then He should keep his promise whether Abraham would complain or not. Is G-d concerned with Abraham's opinion more than He is with His moral obligation to keep His word?

Do you have an answer?

Think! The answer depends on common sense.

> *Hint:*
>
> The source of this *drash*, as we pointed out above, is in the Talmud, tractate *Berachos*, page 9a. If you look it up, you will see the continuation of the *drash*. This should answer the question.
>
> What does it say there?

Your Answer:

Understanding the *Drash*

Answer: The *drash* continues (after the part quoted by Rashi):

> "They (the Israelites) said to him (Moses, after he told them to take the vessels): 'Oh! That we ourselves should get out of here!' This is similar to a man who was in jail and they said to him "we will free you tomorrow and then you will receive a lot of money." He answered them "I beg you, free me now and I'll gladly forego the money."

In light of the completed midrash can you now answer the question?

YOUR ANSWER:

Answer: The parable of the man in jail makes it abundantly clear that the Israelite slaves wanted to get out of Egypt as soon and as sure as possible. They would have gladly forfeited the "great wealth" promised Abraham, just to get their Freedom Now.

In that case, it was not a question of G-d keeping His promise or not, since the beneficiaries of that wealth would have willingly forfeited it, just to escape as soon as possible from their imprisonment in the Land of Bondage. Had G-d allowed them to leave without the wealth, they would have been grateful and would not have complained. This would not be interpreted as G-d reneging on His promise.

However, since G-d wanted to be faithful to Abraham and to the promise He made to him, He therefore beseeched ("please") Moses to convince the people to take the time and effort to take the wealth from the Egyptians so "that the Righteous one, Abraham" would have no complaints to G-d.

❖❖❖

A strange Rashi comment raises a difficult problem.

Exodus 11:5

וּמֵת כָּל בְּכוֹר בְּאֶרֶץ מִצְרַיִם מִבְּכוֹר פַּרְעֹה הַיֹּשֵׁב עַל כִּסְאוֹ עַד בְּכוֹר הַשִּׁפְחָה אֲשֶׁר אַחַר הָרֵחָיִם, וְכֹל בְּכוֹר בְּהֵמָה.

עַד בכור השבי. למה לקו השבויים? כדי שלא יאמרו יראתם תבעה עלבונם והביאה פרעונות על מצרים.

Unto the firstborn of the captive. *Rashi:* Why were the captives smitten (for they had not enslaved the Israelites)? In order that they may not say that their god had claimed satisfaction for the humiliation imposed upon them and had brought this punishment upon the Egyptians.

WHAT IS THE TORAH VERSE SAYING? _____

The verse is basically saying that Moses is warning Pharaoh that *every* firstborn in Egypt will die in the plague. This is expressed by the words "from the firstborn of Pharaoh ...to the firstborn of the maidservant..." Pharaoh being the highest on the social hierarchy, the maidservant being the lowest.

What Is Rashi Saying?

Rashi explains why the firstborn of the captives were also smitten in the plague. When we look further on in the *parashah*, we find that indeed the captive's firstborn was also killed. See Exodus 12:29 where it says:

וַיְהִי בַחֲצִי הַלַּיְלָה וַה' הִכָּה כָל בְּכוֹר בְּאֶרֶץ מִצְרַיִם מִבְּכֹר פַּרְעֹה
הַיֹּשֵׁב עַל כִּסְאוֹ עַד **בְּכוֹר הַשְּׁבִי אֲשֶׁר בְּבֵית הַבּוֹר** וְכֹל בְּכוֹר בְּהֵמָה.

"And it came to pass at midnight that *Hashem* smote all the firstborn in the land of Egypt from the firstborn of Pharaoh that sat on his throne unto the **firstborn of the captive in the dungeon**, and all the firstborn animals."

Now we can question Rashi. The question here is too obvious to elaborate on. Just compare the *dibbur hamaschil* with our verse.

Your Question:

Questioning Rashi

A Question: The words Rashi quotes don't appear in our verse! They are only found in 12:29 where the implementation of the plague is described.

Thus the big problem here is why does Rashi comment on words that appear in another verse but not in the one he is commenting on. This is unlike Rashi. Why would he do it here?

There does not seem to be any easy way out of this problem. For example, it would be convenient to say that this is a printer's error, who accidentally transferred Rashi's comment on verse 12:29 to our verse. But this is unlikely since all the early editions of Rashi have this comment just as we have it. The early supercommentaries on Rashi also deal with this question, which indicates that this text goes back a long time, increasing the likelihood of this being Rashi's own comment. So we have a real problem!

Attempts at Understanding Rashi

In the social hierarchy, the captive is even lower than the maidservant. So why wasn't he mentioned in our verse ?

The commentators suggest an answer. When Moses warned Pharaoh about the upcoming plague, there was no need to tell him that the captive's firstborn would also be slain. The warning was intended to frighten Pharaoh into submission; being told that the non-Egyptian captive would die would have no effect on Pharaoh. For this reason Moses didn't mention it. That non-Egyptians would also be slain is actually hinted at in our verse. If you noticed, our verse says "every firstborn *in the land of Egypt...*" and not "every firstborn Egyptian." This explains why the actual plague affected the captive even though he was not mentioned explicitly in the warning.

In light of the above, some commentators suggest that this is precisely the reason that Rashi inserts here his comment on the captive's son. The Torah verse tells us that all the firstborn were killed, from Pharaoh down to the maidservant's son, but in fact, the captive, who is lower than the maidservant, was also killed. Why? Rashi thus sees the need to anticipate the problem (even before we come to verse 12:29) and tells us here the reason why they too suffered the plague. The reason the captives were also punished was not because they made the Israelites suffer but because if they weren't killed they would claim that their god delivered this plague.

In the Silbermann *English Rashi Commentary*, he offers this note:

"We suggest that the proper place for this comment is after the Rashi comment on מבכור פרעה [previously, on this verse], which explains why the firstborn sons of the handmaidens were smitten. After having given a reason for this, it would be quite natural for any expositor to raise the question: but as a matter of fact Scripture relates that the firstborn sons of captive women were also smitten and these were not Egyptians. Why was this?" Then comes Rashi's comment on "the firstborn of the captive" to explain this.

The meaning of p'shuto shel mikra *is exemplified in this comment.*

Exodus 12:2

הַחֹדֶשׁ הַזֶּה לָכֶם רֹאשׁ חֳדָשִׁים רִאשׁוֹן הוּא לָכֶם לְחָדְשֵׁי הַשָּׁנָה.

הַחֹדֶשׁ הַזֶּה. הראהו לבנה בחדושה ואמר לו כשהירח מתחדש
יהיה לך ראש חודש. ואין מקרא יוצא מידי פשוטו על חדש
ניסן אמר לו זה, יהיה ראש לסדר מנין החדשים שיהי אייר
קרוי שני סיון שלישי.

This month. *Rashi:* He [G-d] showed him [Moses] the
moon in its renewal and said to him "when the moon re-
news itself it will be the beginning of the month for you."
But the verse does not depart from its simple meaning
(*p'shuto*), He really spoke to him about the month of
Nisan: This [month] shall be the beginning of the order
of the months, so that Iyar is called the second, Sivan, the
third.

Rashi offers two interpretations, one is considered *p'shat* (the second interpretation) and one is *drash* (the first interpretation). What would you ask here?

YOUR QUESTION:

QUESTIONING RASHI

Questions: Rashi offers both a *drash* and a *p'shat* interpretation.

Why the need for the *drash*?

Why the need for both?

What's bothering Rashi?

YOUR ANSWER:

WHAT IS BOTHERING RASHI?

An Answer: The verse appears to repeat itself. It says: "This month shall be for
you the first of the months" then it repeats "it shall be for you the
first of the months of the year." Why this repetition? This is probably what is bothering Rashi.

How does Rashi deal with this problem?

YOUR ANSWER:

UNDERSTANDING RASHI _____

An Answer: The *drash* interprets the first part of the sentence in a completely
different way than does our translation above. It does not refer to
Nisan as being the first month but rather sees that these words are
a lesson for Moses in how to determine when a new month begins.
According to the *drash*, the first part of the verse indicates that
G-d showed Moses the new moon in the sky to show him what the
new moon looks like when it should be declared a new month. The
second half of the verse, on the other hand, tells us that this particular new moon which Moses is seeing, is the first month of the
calendar year. In this way there is no repetition, since the two parts
of the verse tell us two different things.

But if this answers the difficulty, why does Rashi see the need to offer a second
interpretation, which he terms *p'shat*?

YOUR ANSWER:

THE NEED FOR THE *P'SHAT* INTERPRETATION _____

An Answer: Rashi makes this clear when he says that a verse can never depart
from it's *p'shat* meaning. Therefore he must offer the *p'shat* interpretation as well.

The two interpretations understand the words החדש הזה in different ways.
How does the *drash* interpret these words?

YOUR ANSWER:

How does the *p'shat* interpret the words החדש הזה?

YOUR ANSWER:

An Answer: The *drash* translates: "this new moon"
The *p'shat* translates: "this month."

Why is the second considered by Rashi to be the *p'shat* more so than his first
interpretation?

Hint:

Where else in the Torah (and in this *parasha*) is the word חדש used? What does it mean there?

YOUR ANSWER:

WHAT IS *P'SHAT,* WHAT IS *DRASH?*

An Answer: The word חדש is found many times in the Torah and it always means "month." In our *parasha* for example we have (Exodus 13:4) בחדש האביב, "in the month of spring". So the simple meaning of these words in our verse is most likely "this month" and not "this new moon." That is the reason that Rashi's second interpretation is considered *p'shat.*

However, it should be mentioned that the word חדש does appear in the Tanach with the meaning of "new moon." See for example the story of David and Jonathan in Samuel I 20:5. where the word is used to mean the "*Rosh Chodesh.*" It is also found in Isaiah 1:13 where it refers the to holiday of *Rosh Chodesh.*

But, while the word can also mean "new moon," since this is never its meaning in the Chumash, Rashi probably didn't consider that meaning to be *p'shat* in our verse.

A CLOSER LOOK

If we take a closer look at Rashi's words we can detect another reason why Rashi's second interpretation is *p'shat* while the first is not. Can you detect the reason?

YOUR ANSWER:

An Answer: The *drash* says in effect "This is what the New Moon looks like." But if so, then the verse should say:

החדש הזה ראש חודש

and not as it actually does:

החדש הזה ראש חדשים

The use of the plural strongly supports the *p'shat* interpretation and not the *drash.* See how Rashi tells us this. In the *drash* he says:

יהיה לך ראש חודש

while in the *p'shat* interpretation he says:

יהיה ראש לסדר מנין החדשים.

Since the verse says חדשים "months," the second interpretation is closer to the meaning of the Torah's words.

(SEE Liphshuto shel Rashi)

❖❖❖

A subtle one-word comment that highlights the drama of the text.

Exodus 12:30

וַיָּקָם פַּרְעֹה לַיְלָה הוּא וְכָל עֲבָדָיו וְכָל מִצְרַיִם וַתְּהִי צְעָקָה גְדֹלָה בְּמִצְרָיִם כִּי אֵין בַּיִת אֲשֶׁר אֵין שָׁם מֵת.

 ויקם פרעה: ממטתו.

And Pharaoh arose: *Rashi:* from his bed.

You must have a question here!

YOUR QUESTION:

QUESTIONING RASHI

A Question: At first glance this looks like a strange comment. On the one hand, this is such a mundane piece of information (that Pharaoh got up from his bed, after all, it was the middle of the night, were else would he get up from?!), we would ask: Why does Rashi trouble himself to tell us this? A second question would be: What difference does it make?

We note that this is a very brief comment. It looks like a Type II comment, meaning that it's purpose is to help us clarify matters. We won't ask "What's bothering Rashi?"

Rather we'd ask: "What is Rashi clarifying?"

YOUR ANSWER:

What Is Rashi Clarifying?

An Answer: Here is a subtle point. The word ויקם in Hebrew literally means "and he rose up" but frequently it is used to indicate the beginning of another action. As in Genesis 4:8 where it says: "And Cain rose up against Abel his brother and killed him." Or in Exodus 2:17 when Moses meets Yisro's daughters at the well, it says: "And Moses rose up and saved them, etc." In these, and many similar cases, the word ויקם does *not* mean to rise up to a standing position. Rather it means that one initiates an action. Rashi, being sensitive to this use of the word ויקם and seeing that no other verb follows, draws his deduction that here it means literally to stand up. Thus his comment.

How does his comment clarify the use of the word ויקם here?

Your Answer:

Understanding Rashi

Answer: Rashi points out that here the word *is* to be taken literally, i.e., that Pharaoh actually, physically, arose. From where? From his bed, naturally.

What about our second question: What difference does all this make? Why must Rashi, and the Torah, tell us this trivial fact?

Your Answer:

The Torah's Message

An Answer: The sense one gets when one pictures Pharaoh jumping out of his warm, secure, King-size bed in the middle of the night, is one of all-consuming panic and confusion. See the other Rashi-comments on this verse and we see clearly that Pharaoh was terror stricken by the outcry from all these sudden deaths. The Torah, with Rashi's help, quietly conveys this message by mentioning that "Pharaoh arose *from his bed* at night..."

While literary style is not the Torah's purpose, it certainly makes use of style in a most sophisticated way to convey its messages.

(See *Be'er Yitzchak*)

Rashi's precise choice of words is illustrated in this comment.

Exodus 12:35

וּבְנֵי יִשְׂרָאֵל עָשׂוּ כִּדְבַר מֹשֶׁה וַיִּשְׁאֲלוּ מִמִּצְרַיִם כְּלֵי כֶסֶף וּכְלֵי זָהָב וּשְׂמָלֹת.

וּשְׂמָלֹת. אַף הֵן הָיוּ חֲשׁוּבוֹת לָהֶם מִן הַכֶּסֶף וּמִן הַזָּהָב, וְהַמְּאוּחָר בְּפָסוּק חָשׁוּב.

And Garments. *Rashi:* These were even more valued by them than the silver and than the gold. The later a thing is mentioned in the verse the more valued it is.

WHAT IS RASHI SAYING?

Rashi concludes that the later a thing is mentioned, the more valuable it is. Therefore, since the garments were mentioned after silver and gold they were considered even more valuable.

What would you ask?

YOUR QUESTION:

QUESTIONING RASHI

An obvious question is: Who says so? Why should we say that the *later* a thing is mentioned the more valuable it is? One could say just the opposite—more valuable things are mentioned first.

What's bothering Rashi?

> *Hint:*
>
> Look at the verse again.

YOUR ANSWER:

WHAT IS BOTHERING RASHI?

An Answer: Of course, logic says that the first mentioned object is the most valuable, but if so, why does this verse say "vessels of silver and vessels of gold" ? Gold is certainly more valuable than silver, yet it comes *after* silver. Rashi is bothered by the unusual order here.

How does he understand the verse?

YOUR ANSWER:

UNDERSTANDING RASHI

Rashi deduces that since gold is only mentioned *after* silver, the order in this verse is reversed. Thus the direction is: most valuable object placed last, least valued placed first and all others in ascending order.

These three objects are mentioned somewhere else in the Tanach, albeit in a different context. Let us compare our verse with that in Zacharia 14:14. There we find the following:

וְגַם יְהוּדָה תִּלָּחֵם בִּירוּשָׁלָָם וְאֻסַּף חֵיל כָּל הַגּוֹיִם סָבִיב זָהָב וָכֶסֶף וּבְגָדִים לָרֹב מְאֹד.

"Also Judah will wage war against Jerusalem; and the wealth of all the nations around will be gathered—*gold and silver and garments* in great abundance."

This order is reasonable. The most valuable first (gold) the next valuable (silver) next, and the least valuable (garments) last.

Why, then, in our verse is the order reversed? Can you think of an explanation?

YOUR ANSWER:

UNDERSTANDING THE WORD ORDER

An Answer: Perhaps the reason is that since the Children of Israel were fleeing Egypt for a trek in the desert, those things ordinarily valuable would take second place to things of practical value. Having clothes in the desert would be of more survival value to them than trinkets of gold or silver.

A CLOSER LOOK

Notice Rashi's last words: "The later a thing is mentioned in the verse, the more valued it is." This recalls another Rashi-comment in Genesis where he also tells us that the later mentioned is the most beloved. Do you know where that Rashi-comment is?

YOUR ANSWER:

Answer: In Genesis 33 the Torah describes Jacob's meeting with his brother Esau twenty two years after he fled from him. Jacob is apprehensive about how his brother will receive him. In 33:2 we are told how he arranges his entourage for the fateful encounter. The Torah says:

וַיָּשֶׂם אֶת הַשְּׁפָחוֹת וְאֶת יַלְדֵיהֶן רִאשֹׁנָה וְאֶת לֵאָה וִילָדֶיהָ אַחֲרֹנִים וְאֶת רָחֵל וְאֶת יוֹסֵף אַחֲרֹנִים.

And he [Jacob] put the handmaidens and their children first and Leah and her children later and Rachel and Joseph last.

On this verse Rashi has a short comment which has become a famous saying. His comment:

אחרון, אחרון חביב.

The very last is most beloved.

The concept seems to be the same as Rashi's words on our verse "The later in the verse is the more important." Why didn't Rashi use the same phrase here as he used in Genesis?

Is there any difference between the two ? What?

YOUR ANSWER:

RASHI'S CHOICE OF WORDS _____

An Answer: In Genesis we are told how Jacob arranged his family, his four wives and their children, when they went to meet Esau. Because Jacob was fearful that Esau might avenge his having taken the blessings (Genesis 27:41) and might attack the members of his family, for that reason Jacob protected his most beloved relatives by placing them further back in the procession. The further back they were, was an indication how much Jacob loved them. The order in the verse reflects the exact order in which they were lined up in the group. Thus: אחרון, אחרון חביב.

In our verse, on the other hand, the Torah enumerates the objects which the Israelites took from the Egyptians. The order of the words in our verse does *not* indicate the order in which these objects were actually taken. Throughout Egypt the Israelites took what their Egyptian neighbors gave them, without regard to which was given first, second or last. Yet the order of the words in our verse (silver, gold and garments) is not arbitrary; while it does not indicate the order of events, the Torah orders the words in this way to convey the relative importance of the objects in the eyes of the Israelites. It is for this reason that Rashi says "the later *in the verse*, the more important (and not *the more beloved*) it is."

Again we are witness to Rashi's precise choice of words in his commentary.

Rashi and Ramban argue over essentials.

Exodus 13:8

וְהִגַּדְתָּ לְבִנְךָ בַּיּוֹם הַהוּא לֵאמֹר בַּעֲבוּר זֶה עָשָׂה הי לִי בְּצֵאתִי מִמִּצְרָיִם.

בעבור זה. בעבור שאקיים מצותיו כגון פסח מצה ומרור הללו.
For the sake of this. *Rashi:* For the sake that I should carry out His commandments, such as the Passover offering, the unleavened bread and these bitter herbs.

WHAT IS RASHI SAYING?

The verse says: The father is telling his son: "For the sake of this [זה], *Hashem* acted on my behalf when I went out of Egypt." Rashi bases his comment on the meaning of the word "זה". According to Rashi, the word זה always designates something visible (see Rashi's comments on Exodus 12:2 "This month is for you the first of the months.." and Exodus 15:2 "This is my G-d and I will glorify Him"...).

Note that the beginning of this verse says, "And you will tell your son on *that day* ..." Which day is referred to here?

YOUR ANSWER:

An Answer: "That day" is Passover when the Jew sits down with his children and recounts the story of the Exodus from Egypt. He does this at the Passover Seder when the *matzo*, bitter herbs and Pascal lamb are in front of him. Thus Rashi concludes that when the father tells his son: "It is for the sake of *this*..." the word "this" refers to something visible, i.e., the *matzo*, bitter herbs and Pascal lamb.

In light of this, Rashi explains this verse: It tells us that we should tell our sons "it is because of this זה, i.e., the *matzos* (and associated commandments like bitter herbs and Passover offering) which we are commanded to eat on Passover, that G-d took us out of Egypt.

Having understood what he said, we can now question Rashi.

YOUR QUESTION:

QUESTIONING RASHI

A Question: Isn't this a strange comment? How could the *purpose* of the Exodus and the attendant miracles done for the Israelites when they left Egypt be *in order that* they keep the commandments of bitter herbs, unleavened bread etc.? These *mitzvos* are symbolic of what happened to us in Egypt. Common sense would lead to the opposite conclusion—that we keep these *mitzvos* in order to commemorate the events in Egypt. Rashi seems to have it all backwards!

What's bothering Rashi?

YOUR ANSWER:

WHAT IS BOTHERING RASHI?

An Answer: The word בעבור means "in order to" or "for the sake of." It does not mean, as we might have expected here, "because of." The word בעבור is used to tell us the goal of an action. If, on the other hand, the Torah wanted to tell us the preceding cause that led to these *mitzvos*, it should have used the word בגלל which means "because of." Then the verse would imply: I eat matzos, the Pascal lamb and bitter herbs, "Because of what *Hashem* did for me when I left Egypt."

A fine example of the difference between these two words can be found in Genesis 12:13, where Avram asks Sarai his wife to say she is his sister (and not his wife). There it says:

אִמְרִי נָא אֲחֹתִי אָתְּ לְמַעַן יִיטַב לִי בַעֲבוּרֵךְ וְחָיְתָה נַפְשִׁי בִּגְלָלֵךְ.

"Please say that you are my sister so that it will go well with me **for your sake**, and my life will be spared **because of you**."

But our verse has בעבור and not בגלל thus Rashi must interpret it as he does. With this understanding of the correct meaning of the word בעבור we can understand Rashi's unusual comment.

UNDERSTANDING RASHI

By translating this verse correctly, Rashi is forced to look for the *goal* of the Exodus (and not the *cause* of the commandments of Passover). The word זה directs our attention to the *mitzvos* which are right in front of us as we speak these words; they are the goal of the Exodus.

Nevertheless it does seem strange to conclude that we were subjected to the bitter enslavement in Egypt in order that we may, one day, be commanded to eat bitter herbs! But if we look closely at Rashi's words we can understand his intention more correctly. Rashi adds one word which clarifies the matter. Can you see which word he adds ?

YOUR ANSWER:

A CLOSER LOOK

An Answer: Rashi says כגון *"for example* matzos, bitter herbs, etc." We see that he means *all* the mitzvos; matzos, bitter herbs and the Pascal offering are just examples of all the commandments which *Hashem* gave us. Of course, these specific *mitzvos* are cited because these are what the father points to when he answers his son's question at the Seder.

THE RAMBAN'S ARGUMENT WITH THIS VIEW

The Ramban takes issue with Rashi's view. He quotes the Ibn Ezra whose interpretation is the same as Rashi's. (For some reason the Ramban does not mention Rashi in his comment.) The Ramban offers his own interpretation of these words. He adds just one letter to this verse and in so doing he changes its whole meaning and avoids the awkwardness of Rashi's interpretation. The Ramban writes:

בעבור זה **שעשה** הי לי בצאתי ממצרים . . . יאמר כי בעבור זה
שעשה הי לי בצאתי ממצרים אני עובד את העבודה הזאת. . .
ואמר זה כלומר תגיד לו שאתה רואה בעיניך שעשה הי לך בצאתך
ממצרים.

"It is because of this *which* Hashem *did* for me when I went out of Egypt.... The father is thus saying [to his son]: It is because of that which *Hashem* did for me when I came forth from Egypt that I observe this service. ...The intent of the word זה is: "to tell him 'that' which you yourself see, i.e., what *Hashem* did for you when you went out of Egypt."

What letter did he add?

YOUR ANSWER:

Answer: He added the letter ש and placed it before the word עשה. The translation then becomes: "*which* Hashem did for me, etc." The verse now means: And you shall tell your son on that day, saying: [I do all these commandments] *because of that which* Hashem did for me when I went out of Egypt.

The Ramban goes on to say:

"Rabbi Abraham [Ibn Ezra] said the meaning of the verse is: Because of that which I do and worship Him by eating the Passover offering and the unleavened bread, *Hashem* did for me wonders until He brought me out of Egypt. But [says the Ramban] this is not correct. I will yet explain this verse [later on]."

The meaning of the Ibn Ezra's interpretation, which is similar to Rashi's, is: The only reason I was taken out of Egypt was in order to worship *Hashem,* with these (and other) *mitzvos.*

The difference between Rashi and Ibn Ezra, on the one hand, and the Ramban, on the other, is in the meaning they give to the word זה.

1) For Rashi and Ibn Ezra, זה refers to:

YOUR ANSWER:

2) For the Ramban, זה refers to:

YOUR ANSWER:

Answer: 1) For Rashi, זה refers to the father's *mitzvos*, the example being those in front of him, *matzos*, bitter herbs, etc.

2) For the Ramban, זה refers to *Hashem's* miracles.

In summary: Rashi and Ibn Ezra say: We were taken out of Egypt *in order* to keep these *mitzvos.*

The Ramban says: We keep these *mitzvos because of* all which *Hashem* did for us when He took us out of Egypt.

These different interpretations reflect different attitudes towards the purpose of the *mitzvos* in general. What basic difference do you see between these two views?

YOUR ANSWER:

THE PURPOSE OF THE *MITZVOS*: RASHI (IBN EZRA) VS. RAMBAN ____

An Answer: It would seem that there is a fundamental difference in viewpoints regarding the philosophy of *mitzvos.*

If these *mitzvos* are done to remember the Exodus from Egypt, as the Ramban would have it, then this means that *mitzvos* have a purpose beyond themselves; they are a means either to commemorate (as here), to instruct or to improve one in some way.

If, on the other hand, fulfilling these (and all other) *mitzvos* was the goal of the redemption from Egypt, as Rashi and Ibn Ezra would have it, this means that *mitzvos* are their own justification. Their performance is the ultimate goal of our existence. The fact that they may signify something beyond themselves (like remembering the Exodus) or may serve another purpose (such as self-improvement) is secondary to their own inherent value, of doing G-d's will. In short, *mitzvos* are their own justification. These two viewpoints, then, represent two very different understandings as to the essential purpose of G-d's commandments.

THE RAMBAN'S KABBALISTIC INTERPRETATION ____

The Ramban will frequently add a Kabbalistic interpretation after he has given us his *p'shat* interpretation. This is usually introduced with the words, "By the way of Truth..." Here too he offers a "true" interpretation of this verse. The following is found within his comment to verse 13:16. There he writes:

"By way of the Truth, the verse "It is because of זה 'this' which *Hashem* did for me", is similar to "This זה is my G-d and I will glorify Him." The verse here thus states that it was *because of His name and His glory* that He did for us and brought us out of Egypt."

What is the Ramban saying? Here we enter the world of Sode [Hidden] interpretation; one the four levels of Torah interpretation referred to as PARDES, **P**'shat, **R**emez, **D**rash and **S**ode.

As we said above the word זה carries the meaning of pointing to something, designating an object. The Ramban seems to take this idea to a deeper level of abstraction. The word זה here designates an idea. In the world of Kabbalah, ideas are absolutes. The idea here, says the Ramban, is not just a designation, it rather the *ultimate designation.* That would mean the ultimate essence of existence. What is that? None other than G-d Himself, His essence itself. This is called: His name or His glory or more familiarly, the *Shechinah.*

See the beauty of this interpretation and how smoothly it fits into the verses.

Where it says "this", we will substitute the word "the *Shechinah*"

זה אלי ואנויהו

Becomes: "The *Shechinah* is my G-d and I will glorify Him."

In our verse:

בעבור זה עשה הי לי בצאתי ממצרים

Becomes: "For the sake of *the Shechinah* G-d did for me when I went out of Egypt."

A Powerful Theme In Torah

G-d did all that he did in Egypt, not essentially for Israel, but for the *Shechinah* (for His glory.) In this view, neither do the *mitzvos* point to G-d's deeds in history, nor do the events of history lead us to the fulfillment of certain *mitzvos* for our self-improvement, rather both history and our fulfillment of *mitzvos* have the same ultimate goal: Glorifying the *Shechinah.*

This idea runs like a crimson thread throughout the Tanach. See the Book of Joshua 7:9. When Joshua pleads with *Hashem* to save the Israelites in their battles with the Canaanites he says:

"And the Canaanites will hear as well as all the inhabitants of the land, and they will encompass us around and cut off our name from the earth; *and what will You do for Your great name?"*

The Prophet Ezekiel stresses this point many times. One example can be found in Ezekiel 36:22:

לָכֵן אֱמֹר לְבֵית יִשְׂרָאֵל כֹּה אָמַר אֲדֹנָ-י הי לֹא לְמַעַנְכֶם אֲנִי עֹשֶׂה בֵּית יִשְׂרָאֵל, כִּי אִם לְשֵׁם קָדְשִׁי אֲשֶׁר חִלַּלְתֶּם בַּגּוֹיִם אֲשֶׁר בָּאתֶם שָׁם.

"Thus said the Lord *Hashem*, It is not for your sake that I act, O House of Israel, but for My holy Name that you have desecrated among the nations where you came."

This theme also occurs previously in the Torah. The two times that *Hashem* threatens to destroy the Jewish nation, once after the sin of the Golden Calf and again after the evil report of the spies, Moses uses the same argument to save them.

After the Golden Calf, he says "Why should the Egyptians speak saying: For evil did He bring them forth etc." (Exodus 32:12)" The meaning being that if the Israelites are destroyed in the wilderness then people will conclude that G-d is vicious and sadistic. After the incident of the Spies, Moses says: "Now if You kill this people as one man then the nations which have heard of Your fame will speak saying: Because *Hashem* was not able to bring this people into the land which He swore to them, therefore He has killed them in the wilderness" (Numbers 14:15). In other words, *chilul Hashem*, as people conclude that He is impotent.

Note, that in both cases Moses makes use of the same theme: G-d's name will be desecrated. The ultimate argument reflects the ultimate purpose of existence: Proclaiming and glorifying the *Shechinah*, just as we have in our verse in the kabbalistic interpretation of the Ramban.

We see the Ramban's virtuosity as a Torah commentator. He makes sense of the verse on the *p'shat* level (with the addition of just one letter) and with equal facility, he interprets on the *Sode* level and opens our eyes to the world of Kabbalah and its profound teachings.

(See *Hak'sav V'Hakabalah*)

פרשת בשלח

Rashi and Ramban disagree over the correct interpretation of nuances.

Exodus 13:17

וַיְהִי בְּשַׁלַּח פַּרְעֹה אֶת הָעָם וְלֹא נָחָם אֱלֹוקִים דֶּרֶךְ אֶרֶץ פְּלִשְׁתִּים כִּי קָרוֹב הוּא כִּי אָמַר אֱלֹוקִים פֶּן יִנָּחֵם הָעָם בִּרְאֹתָם מִלְחָמָה וְשָׁבוּ מִצְרָיְמָה.

כִּי קָרוֹב הוּא. וְנוֹחַ לָשׁוּב בְּאוֹתוֹ הַדֶּרֶךְ לְמִצְרַיִם. וּמִדְרְשֵׁי אַגָּדָה יֵשׁ הַרְבֵּה.

Because it was near. *Rashi*: And would be easy to return by the same route to Egypt. There are many *Midrashei-Aggadah* [on this verse].

What would you ask here?

YOUR QUESTION:

QUESTIONING RASHI

A Question: Rashi tells us the people might return to Egypt because the way was near and easy to return. But this is what the verse itself says. What does his comment add to our understanding?

What's bothering Rashi?

YOUR ANSWER:

WHAT IS BOTHERING RASHI?

An Answer: The verse says: G-d led them not by the Way of the Philistines *because* it was near. Ordinarily the nearness of a route is justification for choosing it and not for rejecting it. Yet here its nearness was the reason for rejecting it. This is strange.

This would seem to be what is bothering Rashi.

How does Rashi's interpretation explain this?

YOUR ANSWER:

UNDERSTANDING RASHI

An Answer: There is a subtlety here which is usually overlooked. "Because the route was near". Near to what? Near is a relative term. If it was near to the destination then this is an advantage and should not be reason for rejecting it. But Rashi points out that the way was also 'near' to where they had come from. And thus the advantage becomes a disadvantage, if returning to the place you came from is ill advised. In such a case the nearness makes returning more tempting, more feasible and the more reason to be avoided.

See how Rashi takes the *dibbur hamaschil* and connects it with the last words in the verse: **Because it is near**...and easy **to return** by the same route **to Egypt**." By inserting the words "by the same route", he shows that "the Way of the Land of the Philistines" was a "two-way street" near their destination but likewise near their point of departure. And therein lay the danger.

THE RAMBAN'S VIEW

The Ramban differs with Rashi here and after quoting Rashi he writes:

"This is the language of Rashi. This is also the opinion of Rabbi Abraham Ibn Ezra, who explained the meaning of the verse to be: G-d led them not by the Way of the Land of the Philistines *because* it was near. They might therefore be filled with regret [when they experienced war] and they would immediately return to Egypt.

"In my opinion, [says the Ramban] if their explanation were correct, the expression "for G-d said" would have been mentioned in the first place in the verse, in which case the verse would read "and G-d led them not by the Way of the Land of the Philistines, *for G-d said*: Because it is near, lest the people change their mind, etc." But the correct interpretation is that [these words] state merely that G-d lead them not by Way of the Land of the Philistines *which* was near and would have been advantageous to lead them by that route, *for G-d said*: 'Lest peradventure the people change their mind when they see war and they return to Egypt.' And the meaning of 'seeing war' is that they would have to pass through the Land of the Philistines and the Philistines would not allow them to pass through peacefully; they would thus return [retreat] to Egypt. On the other hand, by going the way of the wilderness they would not encounter war until they were in their own land, the land of Sichone and Og, the kings of Emori, which would be given to them, and by then they would be far from Egypt [with little chance of their retreating to Egypt]."

The Points of Difference Between Rashi and Ramban _____

Rashi and the Ramban argue over the translation of one word in our verse.

Which word?

Your Answer:

Answer: The Hebrew word כי in the phrase כי קרוב הוא.

How does each of them translate this word?

Your answer:

Answer: Rashi translates: "*because* it is near," the Ramban translates: "*which* is near."

The Ramban cites one piece of evidence against Rashi. What is it?

Your Answer:

Understanding the Ramban's Argument _____

Answer: The Ramban's argument is based on a literary consideration. He says that if G-d's rationale for not leading the Israelites by the "near" route was precisely *because* it was near, (as Rashi interprets it) then this would have been part and parcel of G-d's reasoning. The verse then should have said " ...for G-d said [reasoned]: Because it is near lest the people change their mind, etc." and not say, as it does, "because it is near, for G-d said, lest the people change their mind, etc."

Other than this compositional difference, can you find any essential difference between the interpretations of Rashi and the Ramban?

Your Answer:

THE ESSENTIAL DIFFERENCE BETWEEN RASHI AND THE RAMBAN _____

Answer: I can't find any difference. There seems to be no essential differ-
           ence between these two interpretations. According to both of them,
           G-d led the fleeing Israelites by the longer way, and not by the Way
           of the Land of the Philistines, which would have been shorter, be-
           cause He feared that if they encountered war they would return to
           Egypt.

Rashi felt that *if* they encounter war, the shorter way would enable them
to return to Egypt more easily. The Ramban felt that the likelihood of
encountering war was greater by going "the Way of the Land of the
Philistines" and therefore they would retreat.

LESSON _____

We see from this example that the Ramban saw the necessity of refuting
Rashi if he thought the interpretation of the verse was incorrect. Even
though there may be no practical or even meaningful difference between
the two interpretations. Knowing the exact meaning of the Torah's words
is sufficient reason for clarifying the *p'shat*.

"THERE ARE MANY *MIDRASHEI AGGADAH*" _____

This additional comment of Rashi has been interpreted in various ways.
Throughout his Torah commentary, Rashi will occasionally make such a
comment referring to unstated *midrashic* interpretations. The question
is: Why does Rashi mention this if he has no intention of telling what
these *midrashim* say?

If we check the *Midrash Mechilta*, which is Rashi's source for most of
his commentary on Shemos, we will find many *drash* interpretations of
these words כי קרוב הוא. To give the student a sense of these *midrashic*
interpretations, I will cite two of them.

"**Because it was near**—to the oath which Abraham had sworn to
Abimelech, it was too recent, etc."

"**Because it was near**—to the time Canaanites had taken possession of
the land, etc."

These examples show clearly that they are not *p'shat* interpretations.
Rashi indirectly notes them, but does not quote them because they do
not fit into his rules which guide his Torah commentary. See Genesis 3:8
where Rashi makes his programmatic declaration:

"There are many *Midrashic Aggados* and our Rabbis have already collected them in their appropriate place in *Midrash Rabbah* and in other *Midrashim*. I, however, am only concerned with the Plain Sense of the Scriptures (פשוטו של מקרא) and with such *Aggados* that explain the words of the Scripture in a manner that fits in with them."

Note that Rashi uses the same words in our verse as he does in Genesis יש מדרשי אגדה רבים (though in slightly different order). Clearly, Rashi had such *midrashim* in mind, as those quoted above, when he made that statement.

(See *Mizrachi*)

A seemingly banal comment with a meaningful message.

Exodus 14:6

וַיֶּאְסֹר אֶת רִכְבּוֹ וְאֶת עַמּוֹ לָקַח עִמּוֹ.

ויאסר את רכבו. הוא בעצמו.
And he harnessed his chariot. *Rashi*: He himself.

What is your question here?

YOUR QUESTION:

QUESTIONING RASHI

A Question: Rashi tells us what should be self-understood. The verse says that Pharaoh harnessed his chariot. Rashi tells us the same thing.

What's bothering Rashi that he finds it necessary to tell us the obvious ?

YOUR ANSWER:

WHAT IS BOTHERING RASHI?

An Answer: The fact that Pharaoh prepared his chariot to pursue the Israelites is so trivial a piece of information as to be unnecessary to record. He couldn't go to war without a chariot and he couldn't use his chariot without it being prepared. He probably also tied his shoes (or buckled his sandals) in the morning, but that is not mentioned. Of course not. Why then is this equally trite incident mentioned? It should be clear that the Torah does not mention every possible bit of information when retelling a story. It chooses only what is essential and meaningful. So Rashi is bothered by this superfluous statement.

How does his comment explain matters?

YOUR ANSWER:

UNDERSTANDING RASHI

An Answer: By mentioning this "unnecessary" fact, the Torah alerts us to something important. It tells us that Pharaoh, himself, harnessed his chariot. Certainly it is unusual for a king to do such menial work. This is a task which is ordinarily left for servants. But since the Torah went out of its way to mention that "Pharaoh harnessed his chariot", we can be sure that Pharaoh *himself* did this job.

Why is this important for us to know?

YOUR ANSWER:

THE SIGNIFICANCE OF THE COMMENT

An Answer: This conveys to us the depth of Pharaoh's hatred for the Israelites. His profound obsession with pursuing his former slaves is graphically grasped by imagining Pharaoh dirtying his hands as he pulls at his horses, sweat pouring down his face, as he ties them to his chariot, in his race against time to catch the fleeing Israelites.

A NOTE ON TORAH INTERPRETATION

From this example we can learn something of the way the Torah commentators viewed the narrative parts of the Torah. They realized that Torah narration was always guided by a central consideration: What lesson will this story teach? No parts of the story are included just for literary considerations. No detail or quote is recorded in the Torah unless it carries with it a moral, ethical or religious lesson. The Torah never records historical events in all their detail; this would be impossible. A clear example of this can be seen in Genesis 42:21 when Joseph's brothers regret their having sold him. They say: "But we are guilty concerning our brother for we saw the distress of his soul *when he implored us* and we would not hear, etc." The brothers describe Joseph's reactions at the time they threw him into the pit and sold him as a slave, yet when this event is recorded in the Torah (Genesis 37:24), no mention is made of Joseph's reactions.

POETIC JUSTICE

Likewise when the Torah records the apparently incidental detail of Pharaoh harnessing his own chariot, we can be certain that it is recorded for a purpose; we learn of his all-consuming hatred for the Children of Israel which led eventually to his punishment at the hand of G-d. This punishment is faithfully recorded later in the Torah: "When *Pharaoh's horse and his chariot* and horsemen came into the sea and *Hashem* turned back the waters of the sea upon them and the Children of Israel walked on the dry land amid the sea" (Exodus 15:19). Here is Pharaoh, his horse and his chariot, the one he so energetically harnessed himself!

It should noted that not all Torah commentaries view things in this way. The Ibn Ezra, most famous among the "pursuers of *p'shat*" often regards incidental details as just that, incidental details, carrying no particular import. But this approach deprives the Torah of much of its subtle wisdom and beauty. Rashi and Ramban were both acutely aware of the significance of detail in Torah narrative and sought to interpret its meaning.

(See Leibowitz, *Eyunim, Shemos*)

❖❖❖

A typical midrash-comment which has its source in a textual anomaly.

Exodus 14:21

וַיֵּט מֹשֶׁה אֶת יָדוֹ עַל הַיָּם וַיּוֹלֶךְ ה' אֶת הַיָּם בְּרוּחַ קָדִים עַזָּה כָּל הַלַּיְלָה וַיָּשֶׂם אֶת הַיָּם לֶחָרָבָה וַיִּבָּקְעוּ הַמָּיִם.

וייבקעו המים. כל מים שבעולם.

And the waters were divided. *Rashi:* all the waters of the world.

Ask your question.

QUESTIONING RASHI

A Question: On what basis does Rashi come to this extreme conclusion, that not only the waters of the Reed Sea were divided, but *all* the waters in the world were also divided at that moment? What led him to such an interpretation?

What's bothering Rashi here?

YOUR ANSWER:

WHAT IS BOTHERING RASHI?

An Answer: Did you notice that the verse repeats the word "sea" three times? "And Moses stretched his hand over *the sea* and *Hashem* turned back *the sea* with a strong east wind all through the night and He made *the sea* into dry land."

Yet when it describes the division it uses the word "waters." "And **the waters** were divided." This strongly implies other waters, others than those in the sea are referred to.

How does Rashi's comment address this anomaly?

YOUR ANSWER:

UNDERSTANDING RASHI

An Answer: The Torah intentionally substitutes "the waters" for the words "the sea" since the waters of the sea had already been split (see the previous verse, "and He made the sea into dry land"). Thus Rashi draws on the *midrash* to conclude that all the waters of the world were split at that moment. Perhaps the *midrash* assumes that all the world's waters were split, because the definite article is used, "*the* waters" (הי הידיעה) and not just "waters."

(See Gur Aryeh)

Rashbam disagrees with Rashi. Interpreting subtleties gives Rashi the advantage.

Exodus 14:30

וַיּוֹשַׁע הי בַּיּוֹם הַהוּא אֶת יִשְׂרָאֵל מִיַּד מִצְרָיִם, וַיַּרְא יִשְׂרָאֵל אֶת מִצְרַיִם מֵת עַל שְׂפַת הַיָּם.

ויּרא ישׂראל את מצרים מת: שפלטן הים על שפתו, כדי שלא יאמרו ישראל כשם שאנו עולים מצד זה כך הם עולים מצד אחר, רחוק ממנו וירדפו אחרינו.

And Israel saw the Egyptians dead: *Rashi*: Because the sea threw them out on its shore in order that the Israelites should not say: "Just as we have come up from the sea on this side, so they have come up on the other side [of the shore] far away from us and they will yet pursue us.

What can you question here?

YOUR QUESTION:

QUESTIONING RASHI

A Question: Why does Rashi repeat more or less what the verse says - that the dead Egyptians were on the shore?

Is something bothering Rashi? Or is he clarifying an ambiguity?

YOUR ANSWER:

WHAT IS RASHI CLARIFYING HERE?

An Answer: The words "on the shore of the sea" are ambiguous here. Who was on the shore? The Israelites or the Egyptians? The Rashbam and Ibn Ezra say the verse should be read: "And Israel, *while on the shore of the sea*, saw the Egyptians dead." Rashi on the other hand, says it was the Egyptians, in their dead state, who were on the shore.

What can be said in defense of the Rashbam's interpretation?

YOUR ANSWER:

An Answer: It seems to say that the Egyptians were dead on the shore, but we know that the Egyptians drowned in the sea, not on the shore. Therefore the Rashbam and Ibn Ezra transfer the words "on the shore of the sea" to refer to the Israelites.

Rashi does not move these words from their place in the verse. But then he is confronted with the Rashbam's initial question: The Egyptians drowned in the sea, not on the shore.

How does Rashi's comment deal with that question?

YOUR ANSWER:

UNDERSTANDING RASHI

An Answer: After the Egyptians were drowned in the sea, they were thrown onto the shore. There is thus no contradiction between them drowning in the sea and their being dead on the shore. Herein lies the strength of Rashi's interpretation. Can you find support and validity for Rashi's interpretation?

Hint:

See the *dibbur hamaschil.*

YOUR ANSWER:

SUPPORT FOR RASHI

An Answer: Precisely because the Torah says "Israel saw the Egyptians *dead*", and not drowned, this indicates that they were already dead when the Israelites saw them. How could they see them in their dead state if they were in the water? Simply, they saw their bodies washed up on the shore. This is probably why Rashi's *dibbur hamaschil* quotes the verse up until the word "dead" and doesn't include the words "on the shore," because Rashi saw the main difficulty with the word "dead."

All that was left for Rashi to do was to explain why this happened. His explanation puts these facts in perspective. We are told that G-d did this in order to calm the fears of these recently freed slaves, that their former masters were indeed no longer a threat to them.

(See *LiPhshuto shel Rashi*)

A complex comment requires piece-by-piece analysis.

Exodus 15: 26

וַיֹּאמֶר אִם שָׁמוֹעַ תִּשְׁמַע לְקוֹל הי אֱלֹקֶיךָ וְהַיָּשָׁר בְּעֵינָיו תַּעֲשֶׂה וְהַאֲזַנְתָּ לְמִצְוֹתָיו וְשָׁמַרְתָּ כָּל חֻקָּיו כָּל הַמַּחֲלָה אֲשֶׁר שַׂמְתִּי בְמִצְרַיִם לֹא אָשִׂים עָלֶיךָ כִּי אֲנִי הי רֹפְאֶךָ.

לֹא אָשִׂים עָלֶיךָ: וְאִם אָשִׂים הֲרֵי הוּא כְּלֹא הוּשְׂמָה **כִּי אֲנִי הי רֹפְאֶךָ.** זֶהוּ מִדְרָשׁוֹ. וּלְפִי פְשׁוּטוֹ כִּי אֲנִי הי רֹפְאֶךָ, מְלַמֶּדְךָ תוֹרָה וּמִצְוֹת לְמַעַן תִּנָּצֵל מֵהֶם כְּרוֹפֵא הַזֶּה הָאוֹמֵר לְאָדָם אַל תֹּאכַל דָּבָר זֶה פֶּן יְבִיאֲךָ לִידֵי חֹלִי. וְכֵן הוּא אוֹמֵר "רִפְאוּת תְּהִי לְשָׁרֶךָ". (משלי ג:ח).

I will not bring upon you: *Rashi:* And if I will bring [illness upon you] it is as if it were not brought, **for I am *Hashem* your healer**. This is a *midrashic* interpretation. But according to its Simple Meaning (פשוטו) it means: for I am *Hashem* your doctor and the One who teaches you Torah and *mitzvos* so that you will be spared from [these illnesses], like the doctor who says to a person 'do not eat this food lest it cause you to be sick." As it says 'It will be a healing for your navel' (Proverbs 3:8).

WHAT IS RASHI SAYING?

This comment is like a complex molecule; each part must be analyzed individually. It contains two comments, one *midrash* and one *p'shat*. The *midrashic* interpretation says that G-d will act as a healer to remove any illnesses that you may have. The *p'shat* interpretation says that G-d will act as doctor by preventing illnesses. In the first interpretation, Rashi weaves his comment in between the words of the Torah, i.e., between "I will not bring upon you" and "for I am *Hashem* your healer."

Read the verse carefully.

Now, what questions do you have?

YOUR QUESTION:

Questioning Rashi

A Question: Why does Rashi add a clause ("and if I will bring [illness] upon you") which is not in the Torah verse?

Hint:

Reread the whole verse and try to make sense out of it.

Your Answer:

What Is Bothering Rashi?

An Answer: The verse seems to say, in effect: "I will not make you sick .....because I am *Hashem* your healer." But if the person will not be sick, what need is there for a healer? What has *Hashem's* being a healer have to do with our not being sick? To make the question even stronger, we should note that the verse says "all the illnesses of Egypt I will not bring upon you....because I am *Hashem,* your healer." One need not be a healer to make someone sick. What kind of logic is this?

How does Rashi's comment deal with this?

Your Answer:

Understanding Rashi

An Answer: Rashi supplies some missing words, "and if I do bring [illnesses] upon you, it is as if it were not brought—because I am *Hashem,* your healer (who can cure you)." With the addition of these words, Rashi avoids the illogical connection between G-d being a healer and our *not* having an illness. As the verse is amended, the supplied words connect G-d as healer to the possibility that the person does become ill. Then *Hashem* will heal him.

The addition of these words is not arbitrary. The verse does say "If you obey the voice of G-d, etc., then you will not have the illnesses of Egypt.." The logical deduction is: If you do *not* obey, then you will be ill..." This is what Rashi adds.

But there is still a logical question you should ask about this interpretation. What is it?

Your Question:

A Deeper Question

A Question: The added phrase says that if G-d does make us sick then He will cure us. But if He makes us sick, that would seem to be because we haven't listened to His voice to do His *mitzvos*. If so, why *should* He cure us?

Can you suggest an answer to this difficult question?

Your Answer:

A Deeper Understanding

An Answer: Two answers have been suggested to this problem. One is that *Hashem* will act as our healer only if, after sinning, we do *t'shuvah*, we mend our ways.

Another answer given is that a person may become ill from natural causes, and not because he is being punished for having done some transgression. The Talmud makes a statement to this effect when it says "all is in the hands of Heaven except for illnesses—צנים פחים (*Avodah Zarah* 3b). It is from these illnesses that *Hashem* will heal the individual, if he obeys the word of G-d but is, nevertheless, sick.

How does Rashi's second interpretation, which he calls '*p'shat*' deal with the problem that was bothering him?

Your Answer:

Rashi's Second Interpretation, P'shat

The second comment says in effect: G-d teaches us Torah and *mitzvos* which save us from illness. Here the connection between G-d as Doctor and our not becoming sick is more straightforward. Because G-d is our Creator, He knows the best diet for our physical and spiritual health. As Doctor he helps us *prevent* illness by teaching us the Torah, which is 'our life and the length of our days.' Now the verse hangs together smoothly: If you keep My commandments then you won't have any illnesses because I am *Hashem,* your Doctor, who knows how to prevent illness.

Rashi terms this interpretation *p'shat* and the first *drash.* In fact, both interpretations come from the *midrash Mechilta.* But since the second is closer to the Plain Sense, Rashi considered it *p'shat* even though its source is in the *midrash.* This is really not all that unusual. The *midrashim* are a compilation of the interpretations of the Sages, usually they are *drash* interpretations but sometimes they are *p'shat.*

Why do you think this is *p'shat* and the first is *drash?*

YOUR ANSWER:

A Difference Between P'shat and Drash

An Answer: Perhaps Rashi considered the first interpretation *drash* because he had to add words in order to make sense out of the verse. The second interpretation overcomes the logical difficulty because it makes sense without any changes in the wording. Did you notice that the first interpretation translates the word רופאך as healer, while the second interpretation translates the term as doctor of preventative medicine.

(See *Be'er Yitzchak*)

Rashi clarifies a fine point and in the process leads us to a sad realization.

Exodus 16:4

וַיֹּאמֶר הי אֶל מֹשֶׁה הִנְנִי מַמְטִיר לָכֶם לֶחֶם מִן הַשָּׁמָיִם וְיָצָא הָעָם וְלָקְטוּ דְּבַר יוֹם בְּיוֹמוֹ לְמַעַן אֲנַסֶּנוּ הֲיֵלֵךְ בְּתוֹרָתִי אִם לֹא.

לְמַעַן אֲנַסֶּנוּ הֲיֵלֵךְ בְּתוֹרָתִי: אם ישמרו מצות התלויות בו, שלא יותירו ממנו ולא יצאו בשבת ללקוט.

So that I may test them to see if they will walk in [the way of] My Torah. *Rashi:* Whether they will keep the *mitzvos* dealing with it, *viz.,* that they not leave any of it [overnight] and that they do not go out on Sabbath to gather it.

What Is Rashi Saying?

The verse says that G-d was testing the Israelites. Rashi explains what the test was: whether they would fulfill the *mitzvos* connected with the manna. Rashi does not seem to be dealing with any difficulty here, he seems rather to be clarifying the meaning of the words "So that I may test them if they walk in the way of My Torah or not."

Questioning Rashi

A Question: Why is this clarification necessary? Would I have understood the verse differently without Rashi's comment? What is Rashi clarifying?

Your Answer:

What Is Rashi Clarifying?

An Answer: The verse can be misleading. At first glance it seems to say, "G-d rained down manna *in order to test them* if they will go in the way of the Torah." Does this make sense? Of course not. The manna was given to them to satisfy their natural need for food while in the wilderness, not to test them; yet this seems to be what the verse is saying.

The possible misunderstanding is not so unlikely, particularly when we compare our verse with two similar verses in Deuteronomy 8:2-3. There Moses recalls the manna and the years in the wilderness. It says:

וְזָכַרְתָּ אֶת כָּל הַדֶּרֶךְ אֲשֶׁר הוֹלִיכְךָ הי אֱלֹקֶיךָ זֶה אַרְבָּעִים שָׁנָה בַּמִּדְבָּר לְמַעַן עַנֹּתְךָ לְנַסֹּתְךָ לָדַעַת אֶת אֲשֶׁר בִּלְבָבְךָ הֲתִשְׁמֹר מִצְוֹתָו אִם לֹא. וַיְעַנְּךָ וַיַּרְעִבֶךָ וַיַּאֲכִלְךָ אֶת הַמָּן אֲשֶׁר לֹא יָדַעְתָּ וְלֹא יָדְעוּן אֲבֹתֶיךָ לְמַעַן הוֹדִיעֲךָ כִּי לֹא עַל הַלֶּחֶם לְבַדּוֹ יִחְיֶה הָאָדָם כִּי עַל כָּל מוֹצָא פִי הי יִחְיֶה הָאָדָם.

"And you shall remember the entire road which *Hashem* your G-d led you these forty years in the desert **in order to** afflict you and **to test you** to know what was in your heart whether you would **keep His commandments or not.** And He afflicted you and made you suffer hunger and gave you the manna to eat, which neither you nor your fathers had known, that He might make you know that man does not live by bread alone but by whatever the mouth of *Hashem* does bring forth does man live."

On this verse Rashi comments:

> **התשמר מצותיו.** שלא תנסהו ולא תהרהר אחריו.
> **Whether you would keep His commandments:** *Rashi*:
> That you not test Him and that you not be critical of Him.

Compare the Rashi-comment on this verse with his comment on our verse and ask your question.

YOUR QUESTION:

QUESTIONING RASHI

A Question: Why does our Rashi-comment here pinpoint the very specific and limited *mitzvos* related to the manna while in Deuteronomy he speaks in general of testing the people's faith in G-d? Both verses seem to convey the same message. Can you think of an answer?

YOUR ANSWER:

UNDERSTANDING RASHI

An Answer: Clearly, there is a difference between the circumstances of these two verses. Our verse describes Moses' words to the Children of Israel as they were just to begin to receive the manna; the second verse, in Deuteronomy, is said after the long wandering in the wilderness. It is a recollection of their forty years where their sole sustenance depended on the manna. In this verse Moses tells them that their acceptance of the solitary meal of the manna for all these years was a test of their willingness to uncritically accept G-d's treatment of them.

Our verse, on the other hand, is an announcement that the people's request was being answered. They would have free food. So while they did not receive the manna in order to test them, yet the conditions relating to the manna were to be a test. Rashi clarifies that the words "so that I may test them" do not refer to "I will rain down manna from the heavens." Rather they refer back to the words immediately preceding these words "and they shall pick each day's portion on its day." These are the key words. They could not save the manna from one day to the next; they would remain in perpetual dependence on *Hashem*. Their acceptance of this dependence could be seen by their success in not trying to save manna from one day to the next. Except on Fridays; then they would receive a double portion, for the Sabbath as well. Here the test would be the opposite, they *must* save the extra portion for the next day, the Sabbath, and not go out in search of more manna on the Sabbath.

To summarize: *After* the forty years of eating only manna, the test was if they could be satisfied with this and not complain to *Hashem*. *Before* the forty years (our verse) the test was how they received the manna itself, which at this point in time, they were happy to get, but rather how they kept the rules for gathering the manna. This is the reason for the difference in Rashi's two comments.

A Sad Epilogue

The Torah sadly records the behavior of the recalcitrant people. See what it says in Exodus 16:20:
"But they did not obey Moses and the people left over until morning and it became infested with worms and it stank ..."

And in Exodus 20:27:
"And it was on the seventh day [the Sabbath] that some of the people went out to gather and they did not find."

The only two conditions prescribed for the gathering of this "bread from heaven" were transgressed almost immediately.

And what of the people's attitude to the manna in general. As Moses said in Deuteronomy: their acceptance of it would be a test of their uncritical regard for *Hashem*. How did they stand up to that test ?

See Numbers 21:5 where it says: "And the people spoke against G-d and against Moses: Why have you brought us up out of Egypt to die in the desert? for there is no bread, neither is there water and our soul is harassed by this light bread."

The "light bread," of course, refers to the manna. They were fed up with it. So they also failed the test of faith and trust in G-d of which Moses had spoken at the end of the forty years, when he said "to know what was in your heart, to know if you would keep His commandments or not."

SMICHOS PARSHIOS: An INTRODUCTORY NOTE

There is a *midrashic* interpretive method called *Smichos Parshios* [Neighboring sections]. This means that when one section in the Torah is followed by another, the *midrash* will search for a theme that connects them. The theme is usually a moral message.

It should be noted that while the *midrash* will use the *Smichos Parshios* method of interpretation in a wide variety of cases, even when the sections follow one another in logical or in chronological order. In these latter cases, even though there is no difficulty in making sense of the text on a *p'shat* basis, nevertheless the *midrash* will extract a moral message on the basis of the nearness of the two sections in question.

Rashi, on the other hand, will draw upon these *midrashim only when there is some difficulty* in the Torah's wording or in the order the Torah arranges the sections. This is a clear difference between Rashi's use of *midrash* in his commentary and the *midrash* itself. Remember, Rashi is commentating on the Torah, particularly from a *p'shat* perspective. So only when the *drash* serves the purposes of *p'shat* interpretation, will Rashi cite them. Some examples from Rashi are: "Why is the section of the Nazarite placed near the section of the Sota?" (Numbers 6:2). Or "Why is the section of the death of Miriam placed near the section of the Spies?" (Numbers 13:2).

Again we stress that if the sections follow each other chronologically, we would assume that Rashi would not cite the *midrash*. Logical and chronological sequence need no interpretation. With this in mind, let us analyze the following Rashi-comment.

An important example of Rashi's use of Midrash

Exodus 17:8

וַיָּבֹא עֲמָלֵק וַיִּלָּחֶם עִם יִשְׂרָאֵל בִּרְפִידִם.

וַיָּבֹא עֲמָלֵק, סמך פרשה זו למקרא זה, לומר: תמיד אני ביניכם
ומזומן לכל צרכיכם ואתם אומרים יהיש ה' בקרבנו אם אין.'
חייכם שהכלב בא ונושך אתכם ואתם צועקים לי ותדעו היכן
אני! משל לאדם שהרכיב בנו על כתפו ויצא לדרך, היה אותו
הבן רואה חפץ ואומר: אבא טול חפץ זה ותן לי, והוא נותן לו,
וכן שנייה, וכן שלישית, פגעו באדם אחד אמר לו הבן: ראית
את אבא, אמר לו אביו: אינך יודע היכן אני? השליכו מעליו
ובא הכלב ונשכו.

Then came Amalek. *Rashi:* [The Torah] places this section immediately after the [preceding] verse ("is *Hashem*
in our midst or not?") in order to convey: (G-d's thoughts)
"I am always among you and ready to fulfill your needs
and yet you say 'Is *Hashem* in our midst or not?' By your
life! The dog (Amalek) will come and bite you and you
will cry out to Me, and then you will know where I am."
A parable: a man who carried his son on his shoulders
and went out on a journey. The son saw an article and
said: Father, pick up that thing and give it to me. He gave
it to him; and so a second time and so a third. They met a
certain man and the son asked him: Have you seen my
father? Whereupon his father said to him: Don't you know
where I am?—He then cast him off his shoulders and the
dog came and bit him.

WHAT IS RASHI SAYING?

Rashi, basing his comment on a *midrash*, apparently uses the *Smichos
Parshios* method to connect the attack by Amalek to the story of the Israelites' complaint at having no water (verses 1-7). The attack being G-d's pu-
nitive response to the Israelites' lack of gratitude to *Hashem* for all he
had done for them.

Knowing what you know about this method of interpretation, what would you
ask here?

Hint:

Read carefully the introductory verses of each of these two sections.

YOUR QUESTION:

QUESTIONING RASHI

A Question: If you noticed, the story of the water complaint and the story of the attack of Amalek both occurred in the same place—*Refidim.* So, it would seem that both events happened around the same time, because the Israelites were not in *Refidim* any other time. So why apply a *drash*? The two events are recorded in chronological sequence.

How does Rashi's comment deal with this question?

Hint:

Read Rashi's words carefully.

What's bothering Rashi?

YOUR ANSWER:

WHAT IS BOTHERING RASHI?

An Answer: The verse immediately preceding the story of Amalek (17:7) says: "And he called the name of the place Masseh and Meribah, because of the quarrel of the Children of Israel and because of their trying *Hashem* saying 'Is *Hashem* in our midst or not?'" This verse seems to be out of place. It would flow better if it were inserted above after 17: 2 where it says:

"And the people quarreled with Moses and said 'Give us water that we may drink!' And Moses said to them 'Why do you quarrel (תריבון) with me, Why do you try (תנסון) *Hashem*?'"

Here would seem to be the appropriate place to mention that the place was called "Masseh and Meribah" since verse 17:2 is the basis for these names. Rashi, then, is bothered by the odd location of this verse, placed, as it is, at the *end* of the water story and immediately before "And Amalek came."

Note also Rashi's words: "This section placed next to *this verse!*" Not the usual phrase "Why was this section placed next to *this section*?

UNDERSTANDING RASHI

Rashi's message is clear: Like the boy in the parable, Israel had been continuously receiving G-d's blessings. First there was the "bread from heaven", then the "meat in the evening", and finally the water to quench their thirst. Nevertheless they questioned whether G-d was in their midst or not. Their question implies more than merely questioning His presence. They were "testing" G-d . There were questioning if believing in G-d was worth it. They were questioning whether G-d had done enough for them to merit their allegiance to Him. This is the clear implication of the words "Is G-d in our midst *or not*?" The "or not" conveys their weighing the pluses and minuses of believing in G-d. Besides the obvious ingratitude they expressed, their attitude was one of "religion for profit."

Can you find any basis for the *midrash*'s assumption that Amalek provoked Israel as a result of G-d's desire to teach Israel a lesson?

Hint:

Look carefully at sentence eight.

This is not easy!

YOUR ANSWER:

UNDERSTANDING THE MIDRASH

Notice the first sentence. "And Amalek *came* and made war with Israel in *Refidim*."

In the Torah, when a country *goes* to war, it always says "They went out" as in Deuteronomy 2:32, ויצא סיחון וגו׳ "and Sichone **went out** towards us to war, etc."

Or "When **you go out** to war against your enemies" (Deut. 21:10). This is an *infallible rule* in the Torah (see also Genesis 14:8; Numbers 20:20; 21:23; Deut. 1:44; 3:1; 29:6).

So when the Torah says "Amalek *came*", it almost sounds like he was invited to come! In fact, says the *midrash,* he *was* invited, by G-d, to teach the Israelites a moral lesson! A nuance with a message. One stands in awe of the Sages' attention to fine detail in the Torah's words.

(See *Gur Aryeh*)

Rashi interprets according to the midrash, but in the process, modifies it.

Exodus 18:1

וַיִּשְׁמַע יִתְרוֹ כֹהֵן מִדְיָן חֹתֵן מֹשֶׁה אֵת כָּל אֲשֶׁר עָשָׂה אֱלֹקִים לְמֹשֶׁה
וּלְיִשְׂרָאֵל עַמּוֹ כִּי הוֹצִיא ה' אֶת יִשְׂרָאֵל מִמִּצְרָיִם.

וישמע יתרו: מה שמועה שמע ובא? קריעת ים סוף ומלחמת
עמלק.

And Yisro heard. *Rashi:* What report did [Yisro] hear so
that he came? The splitting of the Reed Sea and the war
with Amelek.

This is a puzzling comment. After reading the verse in the Torah, the
question should be obvious.

What would you ask?

YOUR QUESTION:

QUESTIONING RASHI

A Question: Rashi asks what Yisro heard! The Torah says explicitly what he
heard—"all that G-d had done for Moses and for Israel, His people,
that *Hashem* had taken Israel out of Egypt."

It's all there. Why the need for Rashi to search for what Yisro heard?
Furthermore, why does Rashi state something other than what is stated
explicitly in the verse, like the war with Amalek?

Hint:

Read the verse carefully.

What's bothering Rashi?

YOUR ANSWER:

WHAT IS BOTHERING RASHI?

An Answer: A close reading of this verse makes one aware of several anomalies.

* If it says "*all* that G-d did", why repeat and say "that *Hashem*
took Israel out of Egypt"?

* The first part of the verse has the Hebrew אשר which is translated as "that," while the second part of the verse uses the word
כי, which is also translated as "that."

* The first part of the verse says "all that G-d did for *Moses* and
Israel", while the second part says only "Israel" with no mention
of Moses.

All these points may have been bothering Rashi.

How does his comment deal with these difficulties?

YOUR ANSWER:

UNDERSTANDING RASHI

An Answer: From Rashi's question at the beginning of his comment, we can
understand that he does not think that the verse actually tells us
what Yisro specifically heard *that caused him to come to meet
Moses.*

This means that he takes the word כי, in the second part of the verse, to
mean "when." (The word כי has several meanings. "When" is one of
them; see Rashi's comment on Exodus 15:19). The meaning of the verse
is now "all that G-d did for Moses and Israel *when Hashem* took Israel
out of Egypt."

This new reading answers the first two difficulties: There is no repetition here and the two words do have different meanings.

Since the verse says "all that G-d had done for *Moses* and Israel", Rashi
sought those miracles relevant to Moses (and Israel), thus he mentions
that Yisro heard of the splitting of the Reed Sea and the war of Amalek.
He realized that the exodus from Egypt itself was not for Moses' benefit
since he could come and go in Egypt as he pleased. (Remember, he
came from Midian to be with his enslaved brothers and could have returned if he had wished to.)

A Deeper Look

But we are still left with a question: Rashi specifically states "what report did he hear that *caused him to come*?" Why would hearing this cause Yisro to come, since other peoples also heard these reports and did not come?

YOUR ANSWER:

Answer: The above analysis pointed out the importance of Moses' part in what Yisro heard. And since the verse states explicitly that Yisro was Moses' father-in-law, we can understand that it was the miracles that G-d did for Moses, Yisro's son-in-law, that motivated him to travel the distance from Midian to meet his famous relative. Others who also heard the report, but who had no relationship with Moses, may have been awed by the reports, but they wouldn't have been emboldened to come to meet Moses and the people of Israel.

Rashi and the Midrash

Rashi's source is the Talmud in tractate *Zevachim* 116a. But there the phrase is somewhat different. There it says: "What report did [Yisro] hear and come *and convert*." To this question three opinions are quoted: Rav Yehoshua says he heard of the war with Amalek, Rav Elazar haModai says he heard of the giving of the Torah and Rav Eliezer says he heard of the splitting of the Reed Sea.

Of the three opinions, Rashi omitted Rav Elazar haModai's opinion, that Yisro heard the giving of the Torah.

Why do you think Rashi did this?

YOUR ANSWER:

An Answer: There is a difference of opinion in the Talmud whether Yisro came before or after the giving of the Torah at Sinai. Rashi does not take a stand on this issue. Now according to the opinion that Yisro came before Sinai, he could not have heard of the revelation on Sinai. So Rashi leaves this opinion out.

Did you notice that Rashi also left out that Yisro converted?

What is the reason for this omission?

YOUR ANSWER:

An Answer: If Yisro came *before* Sinai, there was nothing to convert to! The Israelites were still in the category of Bnei Noah, Sons of Noah, like the rest of the world.

Another Explanation for Rashi's Omission

The *Mizrachi* explains Rashi's method in using *drash*. He says Rashi will cite a *midrash* if it is close to *p'shat*, that is, if there is some textual or logical reason for the *midrash*. The explanation of Rav Yehoshua, that Yisro heard of the war with Amalek, is based on the proximity of the war with Amalek (the end of the previous *parasha*) and the beginning of this *parasha*, "And Yisro heard..."

The explanation of Rav Eliezer, that Yisro heard of the splitting of the sea, finds its support in a verse in the Book of Joshua (2:10) where Rachav says, "We heard how G-d had dried up the waters of the Reed Sea, etc." Not also that the Song of the Sea in *parashas Beshalach* (Exodus 15:14-16) mentions how the nations quivered at the awesome news of the Israelites' escape to freedom and the splitting of the sea. So we know that the nations of the world heard of this feat.

On the other hand, Rav Elazar haModai's opinion has little support in the Tanach-text. This is the reason, the *Mizrachi* says, that Rashi did not quote it.

The Lesson

This is an important principle in understanding Rashi's method with reference to the use of *midrashic* sources. He will frequently draw from the world of *Midrash*, but he will shape the *midrash* to his needs as a Torah commentator.

(See *Maharsha, Sefer Zikaron*)

Rashi's comment: a puzzle waiting for a solution.

Exodus 18:17

וַיֹּאמֶר חֹתֵן מֹשֶׁה אֵלָיו לֹא טוֹב הַדָּבָר אֲשֶׁר אַתָּה עֹשֶׂה.

> **וַיֹּאמֶר חוֹתֵן מֹשֶׁה.** דרך כבוד קוראו הכתוב, חותנו של מלך.
> **And Moses' father-in-law said to him**. *Rashi*: By way of honor the Scriptures describe him as "the father-in-law of the king."

Rashi makes himself quite clear here. But if you read through this chapter from the beginning, you will come up with a question on this comment.

WHAT IS YOUR QUESTION?

QUESTIONING RASHI

A Question: From the beginning of the chapter until this point, Yisro is referred to as חותן משה "the father-in-law of Moses" *seven different times*! Why does Rashi make his comment *here*? Why did he not comment on any of the previous references to חותן משה?

Actually Rashi did make a comment on this point earlier. In the very first sentence of this *parasha* (18:1) we find Rashi comments on the words חותן משה.

> **Moses' Father-in-law**. *Rashi*: Here Yisro prides himself on [his relationship to] Moses. 'I am the father-in-law of the king.' Previously Moses had made his own greatness dependent on [his relationship to] Yisro, as it is said (Exodus 4:18) 'He returned to Yeser, his father-in-law.'

We see that Rashi has already mentioned Yisro's pride in having Moses as his son-in-law. Why repeat that again? And if this relationship does need repeating, why does Rashi make his comment on this instance of the reference to 'father-in-law' an not on any of the previous ones?

A difficult question. It has puzzled the commentaries.

Can you suggest an answer?

What's bothering Rashi here?

YOUR ANSWER:

WHAT IS BOTHERING RASHI HERE?

An Answer: I must admit, I cannot think of a reasonable explanation for Rashi commenting here and not previously.

Maybe you can.

Good luck!

I'm curious to know your answer.

A NOTE ON THE SEVEN CODE

We noted above that the words חותן משה "Moses' father-in-law" are repeated seven times in this section. The Torah (and certain books in the Tanach) often make use of the "Seven Code." The Seven Code means that a central word in a particular section will be repeated seven times, or multiples thereof. This is done in an artfully inconspicuous way. The technique is found in each of the Five Books of the Torah. While it usually seems to be merely a decorative insertion into the body of the Torah-text, it serves the purpose of conveying an additional moral message. In our case with Yisro, Rashi tells us that this was the Torah's way of according Yisro a special distinction, i.e., being the father-in-law of the king. For a fuller discussion of this unique characteristic of the Torah, see my book *"Studying the Torah: A Guide to In-Depth Interpretation"* (Jason Aronson Publishers).

A well-known Rashi quote which raises a well-known problem with a not-so-well-known answer.

Exodus 19:2

וַיִּסְעוּ מֵרְפִידִים וַיָּבֹאוּ מִדְבַּר סִינַי וַיַּחֲנוּ בַּמִּדְבָּר וַיִּחַן שָׁם יִשְׂרָאֵל נֶגֶד הָהָר.

וַיִּחַן שָׁם יִשְׂרָאֵל. כְּאִישׁ אֶחָד בְּלֵב אֶחָד, אֲבָל שְׁאָר כָּל הַחֲנִיּוֹת בְּתַרְעוּמוֹת וּבְמַחֲלוֹקֶת.

And Israel encamped there. *Rashi.* As one man with one heart. But all their other encampments were done in a murmuring spirit and in dissension.

QUESTIONING RASHI _____

What would you ask on Rashi here?

YOUR QUESTION:

A Question: How does Rashi know that they were "as one man, with one heart"?

And why does he say all other encampments were with dissension?

What's bothering Rashi?

YOUR ANSWER:

WHAT IS BOTHERING RASHI? _____

Answer: The word ויחן ("and *he* encamped") is in the singular, but since it refers to all the people of Israel, it should be in the plural. Rashi is relating to this.

How does the *drash* explain this grammatical oddity?

YOUR ANSWER:

UNDERSTANDING RASHI _____

An Answer: Rashi uses the *drash* to justify the use of the singular, i.e., that the masses of Israelites were as one, a collective noun—"as one man with one heart."

But this answer is so good that we can ask a question about the *drash*.

YOUR QUESTION:

QUESTIONING THE DRASH _____

A Question: The use of the singular is not at all unusual since "Israel" is a collective noun and thus is referred to in the singular. Why then the *drash*?

What is bothering Rashi that forced him to use the *drash?*

Hint:

Look at the whole sentence.

YOUR ANSWER:

WHAT IS BOTHERING THE MIDRASH?

An Answer: In this verse there are several verbs with Israel as the subject, but *all* of them are in the plural form. "And *they* traveled from Refidim and *they* came to the desert of Sinai and *they* encamped in the desert and Israel (*he*) encamped before the mountain." Only ויחן is in the singular. It is for this reason that it stands out.

A CLOSER LOOK AT RASHI'S COMMENT

Rashi's comment ends with the statement "but all other encampments were with murmuring and dissension." How does he know this? What evidence can you bring for this assertion?

YOUR EVIDENCE:

THE EVIDENCE

See the beginning of this verse itself "and *they* encamped in the wilderness."

Some other examples are: Exodus 14:2 and all the encampments in *parashas Masei* (Numbers chapter 37). Every other time it speaks of Israel's encamping, the Torah uses the plural verb. This indicates that they were not "as one."

"AS ONE MAN, WITH ONE HEART"

The phrase "as one man, with one heart" is a quote made famous by Rashi.

There is a similar Rashi in *parashas Beshalach.* Let us look at it and the problem it creates.

Exodus 14:10

וּפַרְעֹה הִקְרִיב וַיִּשְׂאוּ בְנֵי יִשְׂרָאֵל אֶת עֵינֵיהֶם וְהִנֵּה מִצְרַיִם **נֹסֵעַ אַחֲרֵיהֶם** וַיִּירְאוּ מְאֹד וַיִּצְעֲקוּ בְנֵי יִשְׂרָאֵל אֶל הי.

נֹסֵעַ אַחֲרֵיהֶם: בְּלֵב אֶחָד כְּאִישׁ אֶחָד.

He [Egypt] traveled after them. *Rashi*: With one heart, as one man.

As you compare this comment with the one on our verse, do you see a problem?

What is it?

YOUR ANSWER:

THE PROBLEM: _____

An Answer: Rashi reverses the wording in the two phrases. In one place he says "As one man, with one heart" and in the other he says "with one heart, as one man." Can you think why he would do this? This question has puzzled many students of Rashi. There are two ways to approach a question like this. One way is to think of an answer yourself (or ask someone smarter than you!). Another way is to look up the *midrash* and see what it says.

Can you think of an answer yourself?

YOUR ANSWER:

Let us take the second approach, that of checking Rashi's sources, because we can't think of an answer that isn't overly convoluted. In this case, both quotes come from the *midrash Mechilta*. Checking the sources has certain advantages. You get a clearer picture of what Rashi was looking at when he wrote his commentary. Another advantage is that sometimes you discover unusual things. Let us look at these two *midrashim*.

On our verse, the *midrash* says:
> **"And there Israel encamped**: Wherever it says 'and they journeyed', 'and they encamped', it indicates that they were journeying with dissension and that they were encamping with dissension. But here it says 'and there Israel encamped [singular]' indicating that they *were all of one heart*."

On the verse in *parashas Beshalach* (Exodus 14:10) it says:
And behold Egypt was traveling after them. It does
not say "*were* traveling" (plural) but "*was* traveling" (singular) This tells us that the Egyptians all formed squad-
rons, each [marching] *as one man.*

Comparing the two *midrashim* we see that regarding the Egyptian army
pursuing the Israelites, the *midrash* says they pursued "as one man."
Regarding the Israelites encamped before Sinai ready to receive the Torah, the *midrash* says they were "with one heart."

Can you explain the different language in these *midrashim*?

YOUR ANSWER:

UNDERSTANDING THE *MIDRASHIM*

An Answer: It would seem that in a physical encounter (Egyptians versus the
Israelites) the physical unity of the Egyptian army was crucial, therefore they were "as one man." On the other hand, in the spiritual
experience of Sinai, what was crucial was being "with one heart."
The different emphasis in the two *midrashim* makes sense.

RASHI CHANGES THE *MIDRASH* QUOTE

An Answer: Rashi has done a strange thing. He has changed both quotes. The
one about the Egyptians only says "as one man" while Rashi says
"*with one heart*, as one man."

And on our verse, where the Israelites encamped before Mt. Sinai, the
midrash says "with one heart" while Rashi has "*as one man,* with one
heart."

This is a strange but rarely noticed point, but this is not untypical of
Rashi. He will often shape a *midrash* to suit his purposes.

Why do think he did this?

YOUR ANSWER:

ANALYZING RASHI'S CHANGES

Rashi made slight, but significant, changes in the wording. Where the
midrash said "as one man", Rashi fortified this physical unity by saying

"with one heart, as one man." The physical unity of the Egyptians was supported by the mental unity of purpose. When Israel stood at Sinai, on the other hand, the spiritual unity, with one heart, was central (as the *midrash* has it). Here Rashi fortifies the midrash by saying "as one man, with one heart." The spiritual unity of the people was bolstered by their physical unity.

THE LESSON

Always check Rashi's sources. They can be truly enlightening.
(See M. Kasher, *Torah Sh'laimah*)

Rashi plumbs the depth of p'shat.

Exodus 19:19

וַיְהִי קוֹל הַשּׁפָר הוֹלֵךְ וְחָזֵק מְאֹד, מֹשֶׁה יְדַבֵּר וְהָאֱלֹהִים יַעֲנֶנּוּ בְקוֹל.

מֹשֶׁה יְדַבֵּר: כשהיה משה מדבר ומשמיע הדברות לישראל — שהרי לא שמעו מפי הגבורה אלא 'אנכי' ו'לא יהיה לך' — והקב"ה מסייעו לתת בו כח להיות קולו מגביר ונשמע.

יַעֲנֶנּוּ בְקוֹל: יעננו על דבר הקול, כמו 'אשר יענה באש' על דבר האש, להורידו.

Moses spoke. *Rashi:* When Moses would speak and convey the commandments to Israel—for all they heard from the Almighty's mouth were [the first two commandments] 'I am *Hashem* your G-d' and 'You shall have no other gods'—the Holy One assisted him by giving him strength to make his voice powerful and audible.

He responded to him with a voice. *Rashi:* He responded [to his need] concerning the voice, as in "He responded באש (Kings I 18:24) which means "concerning the fire" by causing it to descend.

WHAT IS RASHI SAYING?

These two Rashi-comments are a pair, they are interconnected and must be read together. The latter part of the first comment (from the words "the Holy One assisted, etc.") is meant to explain the Torah's words in the next *dibbur hamaschil* " He responded to him with a voice." Rashi's explanation to this verse is that the voice referred to here is not G-d's voice but Moses'. G-d *responded* to Moses (and not *answered* Moses, as we might have interpreted these words) by strengthening Moses' voice.

As you read this explanation of Rashi, what question would you ask?

YOUR QUESTION:

QUESTIONING RASHI

A Question: Rashi puts a very unusual twist to the Torah's words. He rejects what would seem to be the simple meaning—that G-d answered Moses with His voice. The Ibn Ezra and the Rashbam, both known as "pursuers of *p'shat*" interpreted the verse in this way. Instead Rashi says that G-d responded to Moses by strengthening *Moses'* voice!

Why does Rashi do this, why does he forsake what looks like *p'shat* for another, apparently strained, interpretation?

What's bothering Rashi?

Read the verse carefully, as Rashi, no doubt, did.

YOUR ANSWER:

WHAT IS BOTHERING RASHI

An Answer: Let us read it as the "pursuers of *p'shat*" read it. "Moses would speak and *Hashem* would answer him with a voice." There are, at least, two problems here:

*   Moses didn't *ask* anything, why should *Hashem* answer?

*   "and *Hashem* answered him *with a voice*" Strange! How else would He answer, if not with a voice? With E-mail?! The word בקול "with a voice" according to the Ibn Ezra's interpretation, is totally unnecessary. Noting these problems, Rashi chose a different path. How does his interpretation deal with these problems?

YOUR ANSWER:

UNDERSTANDING RASHI

An Answer: Rashi's total familiarity with Biblical Hebrew made him aware that
the verb ענה could mean something other than "answer." When this
verb is followed by a noun with the prefix ב, as in our case, it
means "to respond in the matter of." Rashi cites the verse from
Kings as evidence that this is the case. There Elijah is testing the
priests of Baal and says that the true G-d will send down fire to
consume the offerings. His words are "G-d will respond with fire."
Obviously, he doesn't mean *answer* in the verbal sense. He means
"respond in the matter of," Here too, says Rashi, G-d will respond
in the matter of a voice—Moses' voice. In what way will He respond? By making Moses' voice stronger.

When we consider that Moses was speaking to an encampment of several million people, we understand that no normal human voice could
possibly be heard in such a throng. G-d responded to the need of the
hour by making Moses' voice strong and audible.

THE LESSON

What appears, at first glance, to be simple *p'shat,* may, on deeper inspection, turn out to ignore subtle difficulties in the text. Satisfactory
p'shat must take all factors into account.

(See *LiPhshuto shel Rashi*)

Rashi & Ramban disagree over interpreting a fundamental mitzvah.

Exodus 20:3

לֹא יִהְיֶה לְךָ אֱלֹהִים אֲחֵרִים עַל פָּנָי.

לא יהיה לך: למה נאמר? לפי שנאמר לא תעשה לך, אין לי אלא
שלא יעשה, העשוי כבר מנין שלא יקיים? תלמוד לומר, לא
יהיה לך.

You shall not have. *Rashi:* Why is this said? But because
it says "You shall not make for yourself [a graven im-
age]", I can only conclude that one should not "make"
[an image], how would I know that he should not keep an
image already made? Therefore the Torah says "You shall
not have."

WHAT IS RASHI SAYING? _____

This comment, (taken from the *Mechilta*) asks a question and answers it. The question is: Since the next verse (the third Commandment) says explicitly that one is not to make a graven image, why do we need this verse to tell us that one should not have other gods? The *midrash* answers that our verse teaches us an additional prohibition—that mere possession of a graven image is forbidden, even if it was not made by you or worshipped by you.

The logic of the *midrash* which Rashi quotes seems somewhat unusual. Can you think of a question on it?

YOUR QUESTION:

QUESTIONING THE *MIDRASH* _____

A Question: Our verse, "You shall have no other gods etc." comes *before* the verse "You shall not make graven images". If one of these verses is redundant, it would seem to be the second one, not the first. Why, then, does the *midrash* see our verse as the redundant one and the one in need of an explanation?

YOUR ANSWER:

UNDERSTANDING THE *MIDRASH* _____

An Answer: If the Torah had only said "You shall have no other gods", I would have thought this a prohibition against making *and* possessing them. In biblical times, idol worshipers made their own idols. The following mocking remark by the prophet Isaiah is humorous evidence of this.

"It [chopped wood] will be fuel for man; he will take it and warm himself or even kindle a fire and bake bread. Yet he also makes a god and prostrates himself; he makes a graven idol and bows to it.' (Isaiah 44:15–16).

This describes the man who cuts his own wood; part of which he uses for fuel, the other part he transforms into his god and worships it! In view of this, "you shall have no other gods" could be interpreted to mean a prohibition for making *and* possessing idols.

Now when it comes to interpreting our verses we must note a difference between them. Verse 2 ("You shall have no other gods") is vague; "have" in what sense? To make? To possess? To make and possess? On the other hand, verse 3 ("You shall not make...") is more specific, it is clearly and unequivocally against *making* images. The clearer verse becomes our anchor, we accept it as is. Because verse 2 is less specific we have the latitude to reinterpret it to mean something other than "making idols." The *midrash* reinterprets it to mean possession alone. Not only is the actual making of an idol forbidden, so too is the passive possession of one.

RAMBAN'S OBJECTION TO RASHI'S COMMENT

The Ramban quotes Rashi's comment, then he writes:

"In fact this a *Beraisah* quoted in the *Mechilta*. If so this will be a mere prohibition of keeping idols in one's possession, but it would not carry capital punishment. Why then does the lesser prohibition of possession come before the stricter prohibition of bowing down to and worshipping [idols] which is punishable by excision or a court imposed death penalty? I think that the halacha is not in accordance with this *Beraisah,* it is a minority opinion. [The Ramban then goes on to prove that this is the opinion of Rav Yosi alone and thus not the final halacha.]

"The correct interpretation, also according to the *p'shat,* is that this [the words לא יהיה לך] is similar to its use in "and *Hashem* will be [והיה] to me for G-d." (Genesis 28:21). And to "to be [להיות] to you for a G-d." (Leviticus 11:45). This is to say, that, other than *Hashem,* we should have [believe in] no other god amongst all the higher powers and amongst all the hosts of the heavens which are called gods.....This is a prohibition against believing in any one of them and against accepting any one of them as a god or saying of it "you are my god....."

"This second Commandment first warns us that we should *not accept* any master from among the gods except *Hashem* [our verse 2]. Afterwards it says we should *not make* any graven image or picture [verse 3] *to bow down to or serve* them in any type of service in the world [verse 4]. And therefore it says 'you shall not bow down to *them* (using the pronoun)' because it is contingent on making

them [verse 3] and forbids worshipping them [verse 4].
Thus all of these (verses) are prohibitions of idol worship. All of them are punishable by death and there is not
in all this a warning against making idols that will not be
worshipped.....etc."

WHAT IS THE RAMBAN SAYING?

We see that the Ramban disagrees with Rashi's interpretation of this
verse. He mentions three arguments against Rashi's view that our verse
prohibits the mere ownership of idols. What are the three?

YOUR ANSWER:

1)

2)

3)

Answer: 1) Possession of idols is a lesser sin (not punishable by death). Why
then does it precede the stricter commandment of worshipping idols
(which is punishable by death).

2) Why interpret according to this opinion which is a minority view
in the *midrash*.

3) The word יהיה, להיות in this context usually means to believe in,
to accept and not to possess physically.

RASHI VERSUS THE RAMBAN

Can you point out the essential difference between Rashi's interpretive approach
and that of the Ramban?

YOUR ANSWER:

An Answer: Rashi accepts the *midrash*'s interpretation as *p'shat*, that לא יהיה
means "to be" in the concrete sense. You shall not possess images
[they shall not *be* with you]. The Ramban, in a way that is characteristic of his approach, takes the term in a conceptual sense, "Don't
accept" graven images as your god; "don't accept" being a mental
and spiritual acceptance, not a physical possession. We find that many
times Rashi approaches a *midrash* as is, while the Ramban will interpret it in a broader, more abstract way. (See our Introduction.)

❖❖❖

A familiar but puzzling Rashi comment which demands deeper understanding.

Exodus 20:8

זָכוֹר אֶת יוֹם הַשַּׁבָּת לְקַדְּשׁוֹ.

זכור: זכור ושמור בדבור אחד נאמרו, וכן מחלליה מות יומת
(שמות ל"א:י"ד) וביום השבת שני כבשים (במדבר כ"ח:ט). וכן
לא תלבש שעטנז, גדילים תעשה לך (דברים כ"ב:י"א). וכן ערות
אשת אחיך (ויקרא י"ח:ט"ז) יבמה יבא עליה (דברים כ"ה:ה).
הוא שנאמר, אחת דבר אלוקים שתים זו שמעתי. (תהלים
סב:יב).

Remember: *Rashi.* "Remember" [the Sabbath day] and
"Keep" [the Sabbath day] (Deut. 5:12) were said in one
utterance. So too "Those who desecrate [the Sabbath] shall
be put to death" and "On the day of Sabbath two lambs";
so too "You shall not wear *shatnez,* you shall make for
yourself *tzitzis*"; so too "the nakedness of your brother's
wife" and "the leverite brother-in-law shall have relations
with her." This is what is said (in Psalms 62:12) "G-d
said one; two is what I heard."

This Rashi-comment relates to a particular difficulty. What is it?

What's bothering Rashi?

YOUR ANSWER:

WHAT IS BOTHERING RASHI? _____

An Answer: The Ten Commandments are repeated in Deuteronomy, chapter 5.
There, the fourth commandment says "*Keep* the Sabbath day to
sanctify it" and not as we have it here "*Remember* the Sabbath day
to sanctify it." Rashi's comment relates to this inconsistency. (In
fact, there are other differences between the First Tablets and the
Second Tablets, but this is the most glaring and most significant.)

How does his comment deal with this difficulty?

YOUR ANSWER:

Understanding Rashi

An Answer: Rashi, in accordance with the *midrash*, suggests that both commandments, "Remember" and "Keep", were actually said by *Hashem* at the same time; thus there is no contradiction. The Torah, however, could only write one at a time, so in our *parasha* it wrote "Remember" and in Deuteronomy it wrote "Keep." Rashi goes on to give other examples of apparently contradictory commands in the Torah. These, too, Rashi says, were "said at one time."

There are several questions that can be asked about this comment and the *midrash* from which it comes.

What would you ask?

Your Question:

A Deeper Look

A Question: What kind of contradiction is there between "Remembering" and "Keeping"? One can remember the Sabbath and keep it at the same time. The examples Rashi cites, on the other hand, are real contradictions. For example, the prohibition not to profane the Sabbath, includes the prohibition to kill animals, while the command to offer sacrifices in the Temple on the Sabbath day requires killing animals. This is a real contradiction. Either killing an animal on the Sabbath is permitted or it is forbidden. Likewise for the other examples cited by Rashi. But this is not similar to the difference between "Remembering the Sabbath" and "Keeping the Sabbath", which is not inherently a contradiction.

Another question that can be asked is: G-d spoke only once at Sinai, on the sixth day of the month of Sivan, 50 days after the exodus from Egypt. On that day He proclaimed the Ten Commandments. Both what is written in *parashas Yisro* and what is written in chapter 5 of Deuteronomy are a record of the same event. So there is a real contradiction in this sense—either G-d said "Remember" or He said "Keep."

On the other hand, the examples Rashi cites do not contradict each other in this sense since they were spoken at different times. So why are these cited as examples of "G-d said one, two is what I heard"?

Can you think of any answers to these difficult questions?

[We should mention that some commentaries say that the Tablets mentioned in Deuteronomy are the second Tablets that Moses received after he broke the first pair in the aftermath of the sin of the golden calf. But if this is so, then G-d never verbally pronounced them to the people. He only handed these inscribed tablets to Moses (See Exodus, Chapter 32). So there can be no contradiction between what was "said" in the two places, because G-d never spoke a second time!]

What is your answer to our questions above?

YOUR ANSWER:

A DEEPER UNDERSTANDING

An Answer: The Ramban explains the contradiction in the following way. "Remembering the Sabbath" is a positive commandment while "Keeping the Sabbath" implies a prohibition (not to profane it) and is thus a negative commandment.

How can the Torah consider the Sabbath to be, in its essence, a positive command ("Remember") and then later on change this into a negative commandment ("Keep")? In that sense we have a contradiction between the two.

In order to answer the second question which we posed above, we must probe deeper into the meaning of the central phrase in Rashi's comment.

"REMEMBER" AND "KEEP" WERE SAID IN ONE UTTERANCE

This phrase, while well known, is not well understood. This seems to say that G-d spoke in a way that is impossible for humans to speak, i.e., He said two words simultaneously. But if that is so, how could the people makes sense of this simultaneous utterance?

A DEEPER UNDERSTANDING OF THE CONCEPT

The Ramban offers his explanation. He says, in accordance with the *midrash*, that the people heard only the first two Commandments from *Hashem*. The remaining Commandments (including the one to Remember the Sabbath) were only spoken to Moses; he then conveyed these *mitzvos* to the people. So only Moses heard the miraculous utterance of "Remember" & "Keep." It is easier to understand that Moses, possessing his unique level of prophecy, could comprehend the "one utterance."

Afterwards he told the people the two concepts of Remembering and Keeping the Sabbath, one after the other so that they could be comprehended. In light of this, the Ramban makes the startling claim that the word "Remember" was written in *both* the first and the second Tablets! Moses however explained the concept of "Keep" (the negative commandment) as he taught this *mitzvah* to the people.

Still unanswered, however, is our question of how Rashi's examples are relevant to the "one utterance" of "Remember" & "Keep."

Another explanation offered is by one of the earliest commentaries on Rashi, Reb Shmuel Almosnino (1326-1407). He explains that "said in one utterance" simply means that *Hashem* had a dual intention when He gave us the one *mitzvah* of the Sabbath. He commanded us to Remember the Sabbath in positive ways (e.g., making *kiddush* over wine) while at the same time to Keep the Sabbath, in the negative sense, by refraining from doing acts that would profane it. In Almosnino's view, the words Remember and Keep were not said simultaneously, but one after the other, but with one intention behind both. In this way we can fathom the deeper meaning of this phrase.

We can now understand in what sense the examples cited by Rashi are relevant. They all exemplify cases where commandments *seem* to contradict one another. Though they were not actually uttered at the same moment, they were conceived by *Hashem* simultaneously. In the final analysis the meaning of "in one utterance" is that the Lawgiver, *Hashem*, had as His original intention, *both* the positive command as well as the negative command. Thus the examples Rashi cites are quite relevant to the apparent contradiction of "Remember" and "Keep." In none of these cases is there an actual contradiction, for both their positive and their negative commands reflect but one overall intention of *Hashem*.

(See *Ramban, Reb Shmuel Almosnino, and Sefer Zikaron*)

A simple drash with a deeper meaning.

Exodus 20:11

כִּי שֵׁשֶׁת יָמִים עָשָׂה ה' אֶת הַשָּׁמַיִם וְאֶת הָאָרֶץ אֶת הַיָּם וְאֶת כָּל
אֲשֶׁר בָּם וַיָּנַח בַּיּוֹם הַשְּׁבִיעִי עַל כֵּן בֵּרַךְ ה' אֶת יוֹם הַשַּׁבָּת וַיְקַדְּשֵׁהוּ.

בֵּרַךְ . . . וַיְקַדְּשֵׁהוּ. ברכו במן לכופלו בששי לחם משנה וקדשו
במן שלא היה יורד בו.

He blessed..and He sanctified it. He blessed it through
the manna by giving a double portion on the sixth day -
"double bread" ; and He sanctified it through the manna
in that on it none fell.

Rashi's comment is not difficult to understand, but what would you ask about it?

YOUR QUESTION:

QUESTIONING RASHI

A Question: Why doesn't Rashi accept the simple meaning of the verse: The
day was blessed and sanctified? Why does he reduce the blessing
and the sanctity to the one issue of the manna? Certainly we don't
think the Sabbath is holy only because of the manna.

Why does he abandon *p'shat* here?

What's bothering Rashi?

YOUR ANSWER:

WHAT IS BOTHERING RASHI?

An Answer: The blessing and the sanctity of the Sabbath cannot be seen, it is an
abstraction, it has no objective manifestation. Rashi sought a meaning to these abstract words that would give the people something
they could understand.

How does his comment deal with this issue?

YOUR ANSWER:

Understanding Rashi

An Answer: When *Hashem* spoke to the Israelites about the specialness of the Sabbath, He wanted to tell them something they could understand from personal experience. *Hashem* had already given the Israelites the manna. (See earlier in Exodus, chapter 16:14-36.) By means of the manna they saw concretely the reality of the Sabbath, as no other generation has. They received the "double-bread" on Friday which included a portion for the Sabbath and they saw that on the Sabbath itself no manna fell. This was the most convincing way to convey the uniqueness of the Sabbath.

But as you think more deeply about the double portion that fell on Friday (which was supposed to be the blessing for the Sabbath), what question would you ask?

Hint:

Think logically about this, that should help you.

YOUR QUESTION:

A Deeper Look

A Question: Granted that two portions of manna fell on Friday, but one was for Friday and one—only one—was for Sabbath. So what was special about the Sabbath, and what kind of a blessing is this, since it too had only one portion allotted to it?

Can you answer this question?

YOUR ANSWER:

A Deeper Understanding

An Answer: The manna fell each day with enough food for that day. None was left over for the next day. And if someone tried to save some for the morrow, it turned wormy and rotten (see Exodus 16:20). But the "double bread" left from Friday to the Sabbath morning did not turn rotten. So while the Sabbath had no more manna allotted to it than any other day, it was nevertheless blessed. The blessing was that a person went to bed Friday evening with no worry for the morrow, he was guaranteed provision for his next day's meal. This was not so for any other day of the week.

He Sanctified It with the Manna

What does the Torah mean when it says the Sabbath was *sanctified* by the manna's not falling on that day?

Your Answer:

An Answer: The Hebrew word קדוש, conventionally translated as 'holy' actually means 'separated.' It was in this sense that the Sabbath was 'sanctified', it was 'separated' from all the other days of the week in that the people had their food without the need to go out to collect it in the fields. As you think about that, you realize that *that* is what is special about the Sabbath for every generation. The observant Jew need not work for his bread on this day. It is the true Day of Rest. That is its sanctity.

Introduction to Rashi on Parashas Mishpatim

As we approach Rashi's commentary on *parashas Mishpatim*, we must pause. The rules of interpretation that we have been using until now don't necessarily apply. We have stressed over and over that when we approach a Rashi comment, we must ask one of two basic questions: "What is Bothering Rashi?" or, if it is a Type II comment, "Regarding What Misunderstanding is Rashi Alerting Us?" Armed with these questions, we can better understand Rashi's intent and the fuller meaning of his comment.

However, this is not always the case! These questions may not be relevant to understanding certain Rashi-comments. To be fair to the multidementionality of Rashi's Torah commentary, we must be aware of the different purposes in his commentary. In addition to his goal of explaining the Plain Meaning of the text (*p'shuto shel mikra*), he also, when appropriate, teaches us about the legal—*halachic*—teachings of the Talmudic Sages. In this case, his source is the *Midrash Halacha*. This term includes the halachic teachings in the Talmud as well as those of the *Midrashei-Halacha*. These latter are based on four books of the Torah (excluding Genesis). The *Midrash* for Exodus is called *Mechilta*, for Leviticus, *Toras Cohanim*, for Numbers and Deuteronomy, *Sifri*.

Rashi frequently cites these teachings, sometimes verbatim and sometimes with slight changes or abbreviations. In these cases, his purpose would seem to be to give the student a taste of the teachings of the Oral Law and their source in the Torah's words. However these halachic derivations are not based on the Simple Meaning of the Scripture, as Rashi, himself, states occasionally. Rather these are *Midrashic* derivations, *drash* being one of the four modes of Torah interpretation.

The rules of Oral Law interpretation are different from those of *p'shat* and thus, when we study a Rashi comment which is derived from a *Midrash-Halacha*, it is not always appropriate to ask our basic questions. A particular law which was handed down in the Oral Law is not necessarily derived from some difficulty in the text, so asking 'What's Bothering Rashi?' would not be appropriate, it would not lead us to a better understanding of Rashi's meaning.

The classic example of a *Midrash-Halacha*, which is not *p'shat*, is to be found in *parashas Mishpatim* (Exodus 23:2).

לֹא תִהְיֶה אַחֲרֵי רַבִּים לְרָעֹת וְלֹא תַעֲנֶה עַל רִב לִנְטֹת אַחֲרֵי רַבִּים לְהַטֹּת.

Do not follow the majority to do evil. Do not respond with your opinion in a dispute to incline after the majority to distort [justice].

On this verse, Rashi begins a long comment as follows:

לֹא תהיה אחרי רבים לרעות. יש במקרא זה מדרשי חכמי ישראל אבל אין לשון המקרא מיושב בהן על אפניו. מכאן דרשו וכו'.

Do not follow the majority to do evil. *Rashi:* On this verse there are various *midrashic* interpretations of the Sages of Israel, *but the wording of the text does not fit in well with them.* They derive from here, etc.

From this quote we see how, on the one hand, Rashi states clearly that the *drash* interpretations of the Sages is not *p'shat* ("the wording of the text does not fit well with them"), nevertheless he goes on to offer the Sages' interpretations of this complex verse. After he finishes quoting the Sages interpretations, he gives his own *p'shat* interpretation. This shows decisively that Rashi will cite *midrashic* interpretations even though these are not *p'shat*. That being the case, we must readjust our sights when we analyze Rashi-comments of this sort.

I would suggest that in place of asking 'What is bothering Rashi?' we ask the simpler question: 'What is Rashi saying?' This will enable us to understand, in our own terms, the meaning of his comment without necessarily obligating us to search for difficulties in the Torah text, when in actuality there may be none.

פרשת משפטים

Rashi cites an example of a typical, though involved, midrash halacha.

Exodus 21:12

מַכֵּה אִישׁ וָמֵת מוֹת יוּמָת.

מכה אִישׁ ומת. כמה כתובים נאמרו בפרשת רוצחין ומה שבידי לפרש למה זה באו כלם אפרש: **מכה אִישׁ ומת**. למה נאמר? לפי שנאמר "ואיש כי יכה כל נפש אדם" (ויק׳ כ״ד) שומע אני הכאה בלא מיתה, תלמוד לומר "מכה איש ומת" – אינו חייב אלא בהכאה של מיתה. ואם נאמר "מכה אִישׁ" ולא נאמר "ואיש כי יכה" הייתי אומר אינו חייב עד שיכה איש, הכה את האשה ואת הקטן מנין? ת״ל "כי יכה כל נפש אדם" – אפילו קטן ואפילו אשה. ועוד, אלו נאמר "מכה אִישׁ" שומע אני אפילו קטן שהכה והרג יהא חייב, ת״ל "ואיש כי יכה" ולא קטן שהכה. ועוד "כי יכה כל נפש אדם" אפילו נפלים במשמע ת״ל "מכה אִישׁ" אינו חייב עד שיכה בן קימא הראוי להיות אִישׁ.

Whoever smites a man so that he die. *Rashi*: Many verses have been written dealing with murderers and I shall explain to the best of my ability why all these statements have been made. "**Whoever smites a man so that he die**" — why is this written? Because it says "A man who smites any soul." I might understand this is as [even] smiting without death, comes the Torah to tell us "he who smites a man and dies" — he is not responsible until he hits him a mortal blow. And if it had only said "He who smites a man..." and had not said "A man who smites..." I would have thought that he would not be guilty until he smites a *man*. How would I know that one who smites a woman or a child is also liable? Comes the Torah and tells us "For one who smites any soul..." — even a child, even a woman. Also, had it said "He who smites a man" I would have understood even a child who smites and kills would be guilty, comes the Torah and tells us "A *man* who smites but not a child who smites. Also, "whoever smites any human soul..." even a prematurely born would also be included. The Torah therefore says "If one strikes a *man*..." he is only liable if he smites a viable person who is fit to become a man.

What Is Rashi Saying

Rashi attempts, on the basis of the *midrash*, to explain the necessity of two apparently identical verses. He shows how the verses, with their slightly different wording, complement each other, teaching us different laws regarding the situations and conditions which constitute an act of murder for which one is liable.

See how the *midrashic* interpretation operates. No two verses can have the exact same meaning, this would be redundant; there are no extra words in the Torah. With this in mind, the analysis swings back and forth between the two verses, noticing the slight differences between them and using these to enlighten us to new insights regarding the laws of murder.

"Many Verses Have Been Written"

Rashi says "many verses have been written dealing with murderers", and he promises us that he will try to explain them. Yet he discusses only two verses! What does this mean?

This is not easy, can you think of an answer?

Your answer:

An Answer: In fact Rashi does discuss the various verses, but he does so when they appear in the Torah and not here. See Rashi's comments on Exodus 21:14 and Numbers 35:16. Here he just discusses our verse and one directly related to it.

"I Shall Explain to the Best of My Ability"

Notice that Rashi says "I shall explain to the best of my ability..." This is strange since Rashi's source is the *midrash*, these are not Rashi's own interpretations. But it is not all that strange, since Rashi's Torah commentary is based to a great extent on the interpretations of the Sages. So this statement is probably a reflection of Rashi's modesty; as if he is saying, "I will do the best I can to explain this as the Sages do."

A Closer Look at the *Drash*

Let us take a closer look at some parts of this *drash*. Among the lessons of this *drash* is the following: Because it says "A man who smites any soul," I might understand this as [even] smiting without death, in which case the aggressor would be liable to punishment by death. A question we could ask is: How could we ever think that he could be held responsible and given the death penalty for hitting someone whom he only injures but does not kill? The Torah explicitly states further (Exodus 21:18), "When men quarrel and one man smites his fellow with a stone or with a fist and he does not die but becomes bedridden. If he [the victim] gets up. . .the one who smote him *shall be aquitted*." Why then would I ever assume that a non-mortal blow could be punishable by death?

Can you think of an answer?

Hint:

Compare the two cases. Are they the same?

YOUR ANSWER:

An Answer: The two cases are not the same. The case in Exodus 21:18 is of two men quarreling. We don't know who started the fight. Perhaps the killer was attacked and he hit back in self-defense. This, then, may be the reason that there is no death penalty in that case. On the other hand, in our case the Torah speaks of unprovoked aggression; I might have thought that in such a case the aggressor might be liable even if the blow wasn't mortal. Therefore we need the *drash* that Rashi cites to teach us that a nonmortal blow, even if it is unprovoked, is not punishable by death.

The Lesson:

Rashi-comments on *halachic drash* must also be analyzed for their deeper meaning, but in a way different from that used to analyze his *p'shat* interpretations.

(See *Mizrachi, Sefer Zikaron; Be'er Avraham* on *Mechilta*)

An excellent illustration of the different approaches of Rashi and Ramban to p'shat interpretation.

Exodus 21:19

אִם יָקוּם וְהִתְהַלֵּךְ בַּחוּץ עַל מִשְׁעַנְתּוֹ וְנִקָּה הַמַּכֶּה רַק שִׁבְתּוֹ יִתֵּן וְרַפֹּא יְרַפֵּא.

עַל מִשְׁעַנְתּוֹ. עַל בּוּרְיוֹ וְכֹחוֹ.

On his staff. *Rashi:* On his [former] healthy state and vigor.

Rashi takes the words על משענתו 'upon his staff' in a figurative sense. What would you ask here?

YOUR QUESTION:

QUESTIONING RASHI

A Question: The Torah says "he went outside on his staff." Why not take these words literally? Remember the rule, אין מקרא יוצא מידי פשוטו "The Torah verse never abandons its Plain Meaning." We also know that Rashi generally prefers the Plain Meaning, פשוטו של מקרא. Why does he abandon it here?

What's bothering Rashi?

YOUR ANSWER:

WHAT IS BOTHERING RASHI?

An Answer: The previous verse tells us that if man hits another man, but does not kill him, yet the injury causes him to be bedridden, then (our verse) "if he rises and goes outside on his staff", the villain is set free.

But Rashi implicitly asks: Why is he free? Seeing that the injured man is still showing signs of his injury (he needs a staff to get around), he still might have a relapse and die. Why, then, is the culprit free?

How does Rashi's comment deal with this difficulty?

YOUR ANSWER:

Understanding Rashi

An Answer: Rashi's interpretation (his healthy state and strength) avoids this difficulty. It says that only if he the injury is completely healed ("he goes about on his own strength") is the aggressor free.

We must keep in mind that the aggressor is being held as a possible murderer (see the next Rashi-comment "And the one who struck will be absolved").

Note that our verse says that in any case the aggressor must pay for the victim's medical expenses and loss of wages. So the only charge that is in doubt is the charge of murder. How can we absolve him of such a serious charge if the injured man still has not recovered completely? Thus Rashi (and the *Mechilta*) says he is no longer crippled; he walks around on his own, unassisted, strength.

But how can Rashi turn the words of the Torah on their head? "On his staff" seems to mean weak, yet Rashi says "strong."

Your Answer:

An Answer: The word משענת means a support; here the word is "*his* support." Rashi takes the word "his" to mean his own, internal, support and not an external support, which in the final analysis is not really "his." The Ibn Ezra makes the same point by saying that the Torah used the word משענת to tell us the man is not dependent on others for getting around.

The Ramban's Dispute with Rashi

The Ramban quotes Rashi and then goes on to say:

"In my opinion משענתו is to be understood literally [a staff] just as in the verse 'every man with *mishanto* [his staff] in his hand in his old age' (Zechariah 8:4). Scripture is thus stating that if the injured person's health improves sufficiently to enable him to go out walking as he wishes in the streets and in the broad ways with his staff like those healed with some prolonged disabling injury, 'then he that smote him shall be free.' It also teaches us that if the injured man is careless [later] about his health and dies after that, in his weakness, that the assailant is free from the death penalty. Scripture says 'and he walks outside' because it speaks of the ordinary way of life, for injured men who were laid up in bed do not go out walking again until their wounds have healed and they are out of danger, this being the sense of the phrase 'and he walks outside,' because if he just gets up and walks in his house on his staff and then dies, the assailant is not free."

The Ramban continues:

"In the words of the *Mechilta*, 'If he rise up and walk', I might think this means within the house, Scripture therefore says, 'outside.' But from the word 'outside' I might think that even if he was wasting away [the aggressor would be free] Scripture therefore says 'if he rise up.'

This explanation [the Ramban continues] too, is very correct, that Scripture should be saying that if the injured man gets up completely from his bed and goes steadily outside without having to go back to his bed when returning from outside, as those do that are wasting away, even though he is weak and has to lean on his staff, the assailant shall be left off. *In general, all this is to be interpreted as being figurative language expressing people's usual conduct.* The basic rule is that he must have been assessed as being capable of recovery.

Understanding the Ramban

By his final statement it would seem the Ramban does agree with Rashi, that the term "*mishanto*" is not to be taken literally. Yet this would contradict what he said at the outset of this commentary, i.e., that the word *should* be taken literally!

In one word, how are the words "walking on his staff" seen by:

The Ramban?

Rashi?

Your Answer:

Answer: Ramban: as an example.

            Rashi: as a metaphor.

The Ramban is saying that if, in fact, the injured man recovered sufficiently to walk outside on his cane, then the assailant could no longer be held accountable for any future setbacks. This is an example, says the

Ramban, of the kind of a reasonable, normal-type recovery, and therefore the assailant is free of any further responsibility. Walking around outside is but a common example of a healthy recovery from an injury.

So it is both an example and a general rule. The rule, as the Ramban clearly says, is:

"That he must have been assessed as being capable of recovery."

Rashi, on the other hand, says that "walking outside on his cane" is but a metaphor of a complete recovery. But in fact, if the man was still using a cane, even if he walked outside, he could not be considered completely recovered. If he had a relapse, according to Rashi, the assailant *would be* responsible. There is a clear difference in *Halacha* between Rashi and the Ramban.

Two Approaches to *P'shat* Interpretation: Rashi and Ramban

This dispute is a fortunate opportunity to examine the different approaches to Torah interpretation by these two great expositors.

To better understand Rashi, let us see his source. It is in the *Mechilta*.

It says: "If he rise up and walk outside upon his support", that means, is restored to his health. This is one of three expressions in the Torah which Rav Yishmael interpreted figuratively..."

Rashi's Approach

Rashi follows Rav Yishmael that this verse is to be taken figuratively. We can deduce from Rav Yishmael's statement that all other verses in the Torah (besides the three he mentions) are *not to* be taken figuratively, rather in their Plain Meaning, *p'shat*. We know that Rashi is committed to *p'shat* interpretation, but this is qualified by the Sages' view of *p'shat*. This is an important point to understand if we are to fully appreciate Rashi's approach to *p'shat* interpretation. For Rashi *p'shat* is not independent of the Sage's view. *P'shat*, in Rashi's approach, is tempered by *midrashim* which can fit into the words of the Torah. As Rashi said in Bereishis (Genesis 3:8), he is interested in "p'shuto shel mikra *and the aggados that explain the words of the Scripture in a manner that fits in with them.*" In short, the Plain Sense, *p'shat*, interpretation also includes under its umbrella the interpretations of the Sages, as long as the Torah text can accommodate them. In our verse an authoritative Sage, Rav Yishmael, says that the verse is to be taken figuratively and Rashi does so.

This view of *p'shat* is not universally accepted among the *Rishonim*. For example, the Rashbam, Rashi's own grandson, argues with Rashi many times regarding the *p'shat* interpretation of various verses. Many *Rishonim* understand *p'shat* as we might, *viz.* what makes most sense in the context of the verse.

The Ramban views Torah interpretation similarly to these Rishonim and differently from Rashi. He will often argue with Rashi regarding the interpretation of a verse and the argument frequently revolves around what is considered *p'shat*. In our verse the Ramban, while fully aware of Rav Yishmael's opinion, offers a different view. While Rav Yishmael takes the words "walking on his cane" as a metaphor, the Ramban sees the literal interpretation as closer to *p'shat* and does not hesitate to say so. For him *p'shat* and Rabbinic interpretation are two separate realms, they need not be combined nor confused. Rashi seems to combine *midrash* and *p'shat* and molds from them his own type of *p'shat*. He does this out of conscious consideration of the Sages' view. Rashi's only qualification for using *midrash* as *p'shat* is that the *midrashic* meaning must fit into the words of the Torah.

Rashi conveys an important piece of information in a very subtle way.

Exodus 21:19

(Same verse as above)

ורפא ירפא: כתרגומו, ישלם שכר הרופא. (ב״ק פה.)
And he shall heal. *Rashi:* As the Targum translates it. He shall pay the doctor's fee.

This is one example of the more than a hundred times that Rashi cites the Targum Onkelus. What would you ask here?

YOUR QUESTION:

QUESTIONING RASHI

A Question: After Rashi tells us that the meaning of these words is "as the Targum translates it," he goes on to say in Hebrew exactly what the Targum says in Aramaic. This is unusual. Why would he do that? Although we could say that Rashi is telling us what the Aramaic words mean, this doesn't seem likely, because many times Rashi says "as the Targum has it" and he does not give the Hebrew equivalent. Why does he do so here?

What is Rashi telling us?

This is a difficult one. Familiarity with Aramaic is essential.

YOUR ANSWER:

WHAT IS RASHI TELLING US?

An Answer: The Targum's words are ואגר אסיא ישלם. The word אסיא means "doctor" in Aramaic. But in Aramaic grammar there is no definite article ("the"), as there is in Hebrew, where the letter ה serves this purpose. So, in Aramaic, "*a* doctor" and "*the* doctor" are both translated as אסיא. We can now see what Rashi has done. He has clarified the vague Aramaic, by adding the word "**the** doctor" — **הרופא**.

Rashi is telling us an important piece of legal information. That is, that the guilty party, in this assault case, must pay "*the* doctor's fee" not "*a* doctor's fee." Anyone familiar with insurance payments can understand the significance of this difference. The injured man can't say "Give me the usual doctor's fee and I'll take care of the rest." He must, rather, bring a receipt from *the doctor* who treated him. Why is the Torah particular that the victim bring a receipt from a doctor before he receive payment?

YOUR ANSWER:

An Answer: In a case where he is 'healed by *a* doctor' he may say he will go to a doctor but never do so. He may pocket the money himself, not heal himself and eventually the defender would be held accountable.

RASHI'S SOURCE

The Talmudic source for Rashi's comment is the tractate *Bava Kama* 85a. There the Talmud discusses several options the defendant may offer the injured person, instead of paying the medical expenses outright. He might say "I'm a doctor myself. I'll heal you." Or he might say "I know a doctor that will do it for nothing or for very cheap." In both cases the injured man has the right to refuse and demand expert medical care. Likewise, if the injured man says "Pay me the money and I'll take care of it myself" the defendant can refuse and demand that a bonafide doctor treat him. This latter case may be the reason Rashi spells out the Targum by adding the definite article *"the* doctor."

TEXTUAL BASIS FOR THE *DRASH*

While the laws of injury payments (some of which we cited above) are derived by the Talmudic Sages by means of *drash* methods of interpretation, the laws do have a grounding in the *p'shat* of this verse. Can you find a textual basis in our verse for the laws which obligate the offender to hire a good doctor and not just give financial remuneration?

YOUR ANSWER:

SUPPORT FROM THE TORAH'S WORDS

An Answer: The verse says רק שבתו יתן ורפא ירפא. "Still he must pay for his loss of work and cause him to be thoroughly healed." (In English it is glaringly clear!)

Why doesn't the Torah just say רק שבתו ורפואתו יתן "Still he must pay his loss of work and his medical expenses"? By separating payments for "loss of work" from the medical payments, the Torah hints at a difference between them. The first is strictly a monetary matter; the second, a medical matter, the purpose being physical recovery, and not merely financial remuneration.

(See *Sefer Zikaron*)

A typical example of midrash-halacha which is not p'shat.

Exodus 22:3

אִם הִמָּצֵא תִמָּצֵא בְיָדוֹ הַגְּנֵבָה מִשּׁוֹר עַד חֲמוֹר עַד שֶׂה חַיִּים שְׁנַיִם יְשַׁלֵּם.

חיים שנים ישלם: ולא ישלם לו מתים אלא חיים או דמי חיים.
Alive he shall pay double. *Rashi:* He may not pay with dead [animals] but only with live ones or with the value of live ones.

WHAT IS RASHI SAYING

Rashi explains the verse according to the Talmudic law, i.e., if a live animal was stolen and then dies in the possession of the thief, he cannot return the carcass as partial payment and then add an additional monetary sum to make up the difference in value. The law is, if he stole a live animal, he must return a live animal. This is derived by connecting the word חיים "live" with the words שנים ישלם "he shall pay two."

THE *DRASH* METHOD OF INTERPRETATION

The interpretation here is clearly not *p'shat*. Since under the word חיים "live" is the musical note "*esnachta,*" a comma. In other words, the Plain Sense reading is: "If the stolen article will be found *live* in his possession, whether it is an ox, donkey or sheep, he must pay back double." The emphasis of this verse is on the stolen animal being found *alive in the possession* of the thief. This is in contrast to a previous verse (21:37) where it says "If a man steals an ox or a sheep or a goat and slaughter it or sell it, he shall pay five cattle in place of the ox and four sheep in place of the sheep." In this case, the animal is either no longer in the thief's possession or it is dead. The punishment then is harsher.

In any event, we see that the Plain Meaning interpretation connects the word חיים to the first half of the sentence because it is separated from the words "he must pay back double" by a comma. But the *drash* connects this word with the latter part of the verse, giving it the meaning "pay back two *live* animals."

This is a common characteristic of *drash*. The Sages will interpret a verse by taking words out of context or by disregarding the musical notes, which show us how a verse is to be divided up. They do so in order to derive an *halachic* teaching.

When Rashi relies on such *halachic drash* we can no longer meaningfully search for a common sense basis for his comment. We are in a different realm of conceptualization.

A Closer Look

Did you notice the different animals mentioned in these two parallel verses?

In verse 21:37 where the animal is slaughtered or sold, it mentions an ox or a sheep. In our verse (22:3) where the animal is kept alive, it mentions an ox, *donkey* or sheep.

Why would you say the Torah adds the donkey here?

Your Answer:

An Answer: It would seem that if one wanted to slaughter the animal to eat, than only an ox or a sheep would be appropriate. Both are kosher animals; a donkey is not a kosher animal. But if one wanted to keep the animal for work, than a donkey would also be a likely object of theft. The Torah chooses those animals which are appropriate to the situation.

The Lesson

Close reading of the Torah's words is vital to a fuller understanding. The Torah's choice of words should never be glossed over. It is always precise in its wording.

An exquisite example of a deceptively simple comment which makes us aware of an unnoticed difficulty in the verse.

Exodus 22:20

וְגֵר לֹא תוֹנֶה וְלֹא תִלְחָצֶנּוּ כִּי גֵרִים הֱיִיתֶם בְּאֶרֶץ מִצְרָיִם.

כִּי גֵרִים הֱיִיתֶם: אם הוניתו אף הוא יכול להונותך ולומר לך אף אתה מגרים באת, מום שבך אל תאמר לחברך. כל לשון גר אדם שלא נולד באותה מדינה אלא בא ממדינה אחרת לגור שם.

For you were strangers. *Rashi*: If you vex him he can also vex you by saying "you too are descended from גרים strangers." Do not reproach your fellow man about a fault which you also have. The term גר means a person who has not been born in that land (where he is presently living) but has come from another country to dwell there.

WHAT IS RASHI SAYING

Rashi seems to be spelling out in concrete terms what the verse itself says in more general terms. Do not harass the stranger because you too are vulnerable and can, in turn, be harassed by him. Rashi then continues and gives the definition of the word גר.

What would you ask of Rashi here?

YOUR QUESTION:

QUESTIONING RASHI

A Question: What has Rashi added to my understanding that I didn't know before? Why the need for the comment altogether?

What's bothering Rashi?

Hint:

Read the verse carefully and understand it fully.

YOUR ANSWER:

WHAT IS BOTHERING RASHI?

An Answer: Do you understand the verse? If you do, then you can answer this question:

What kind of גר is referred to in this verse?

> Be aware that there are two types of גרים.
> 1) The גר תושב "the stranger-sojourner." He lives in the Land of Israel, but isn't Jewish. He observes the Seven Noachide laws, as any non-Jew is obligated to do.
> 2) The גר צדק "the righteous convert." He is a convert to Judaism and is a full-fledged Jew.

Which גר is referred to here?

YOUR ANSWER:

UNDERSTANDING THE VERSE

An Answer: The גר here is a convert. Rashi's comment is based on the *midrash Mechilta* and the Talmud *Bava Metzia* 59b. The *Mechilta's* words are the sharpest: "Don't say to him 'Until now swine's flesh was sticking out from between your teeth and now you dare to stand up and speak against me!' "

Rashi's comment is based on the *midrash Mechilta* and the Talmud *Bava Metzia* 59b.

So, it is clear that the verse is referring to a convert, who "until now" was eating swine.

Now, do you still understand the verse? If you do you, then we can ask: What does it mean when it says: "for you were גרים in Egypt"?

YOUR ANSWER?

UNDERSTANDING RASHI

An Answer: Certainly our forefathers weren't *converts* in Egypt. They were strangers in a strange land, in a word — foreigners. But if they were foreigners, and not converts, and if the stranger we are enjoined not to oppress is a convert and not a foreigner, what kind of comparison is there? Of what relevance is the fact that "you were גרים in the land of Egypt", since we were a very different type of גר than the one being taunted?

It is for this reason that Rashi defines, at this point, and at this point only, the simple word גר as one who comes from another country. Aware, as he is, of the two different meanings of גר in this verse, Rashi makes it clear what kind of גרים the Israelites were in Egypt.

The relationship between the two types of strangers is explained in the Talmud, *Bava Metzia* 59b. There it says: one should not say to a person who has had someone in his family sentenced to death by hanging "your clothes are *hanging* on the line outside." Just the mere mention of the idea of "hanging" sends chills down his spine, so we are reminded to be sensitive to this. Likewise here: The Torah is telling us to be sensitive to anyone who is a גר, because as long as your status is similar to his, even if in name only, then you too are vulnerable to his taunts and thus you of all people, should be sensitive to his vulnerable position.

THE LESSON

Rashi's internal reasoning may not always be apparent to us, but we can be assured that once we discover it, its logic will be convincing.

Rashi cites an halachic drash which has a basis in the text.

Exodus 23:7

מִדְּבַר שֶׁקֶר תִּרְחָק וְנָקִי וְצַדִּיק אַל תַּהֲרֹג כִּי לֹא אַצְדִּיק רָשָׁע.

וְנָקִי וְצַדִּיק אַל תַּהֲרֹג: מנין ליוצא מבית הדין חייב ואמר אחד יש לי ללמד עליו זכות שמחזירין אותו, תלמוד לומר וְנָקִי אל תהרג ואף על פי שאינו צדיק שלא נצטדק בבית דין מכל מקום נקי הוא מדין מיתה שהרי יש לך לזכותו. ומנין ליוצא מבית הדין זכאי ואמר אחד יש לי ללמד עליו חובה שאין מחזירין אותו לבית הדין, תלמוד לומר וְצַדִּיק אל תהרג וזה צדיק הוא שנצטדק בבית דין.

Do not kill one who is innocent or one who is right-eous: *Rashi*. How do we know that if one leaves the court convicted and then someone says 'I am able to argue in his favor' that they should return him [to court to testify]? The Torah says 'Do not kill one who is innocent' even though he is not 'righteous' since he was not acquitted in court, nevertheless, he is free from the death penalty because you have [evidence] to acquit him. And how do we know that one who leaves the court acquitted and someone says 'I am able to argue against him' that they do not return him to the court? The Torah says 'Do not kill one who is righteous' and this one is righteous since he has been acquitted by the court.

WHAT IS RASHI SAYING?

Rashi explains two halachic lessons which the Sages derived from our verse. The laws are clear enough. They concern what modern jurists call "double jeopardy." This means that once a man has been through the judicial process and found to be innocent he cannot be tried again. But our verse teaches us "double jeopardy" Torah-style. This means that a man cannot be tried twice for the same crime if there is new evidence that will convict him. Yet he can be tried twice if, after being convicted, there is new evidence that will increase his chances of being set free. These laws show the beauty and humanity of Torah law.

But on what basis are these laws derived from our verse? These are not arbitrary derivations. What about the verse led the Sages (and Rashi) to these conclusions?

Or to put the question in another way: Why can't we interpret the verse simply—don't kill an innocent man?

What's bothering Rashi?

YOUR ANSWER:

WHAT IS BOTHERING RASHI? _____

An Answer: Several points have been made.

> * The Sixth Commandment has already taught us that murder is forbidden, why repeat it here?
>
> * This verse is placed within the context of laws that relate to judges.
>
> * What is the significance of the repetition of "innocent" and "righteous"?

These considerations led the Sages to conclude that our verse should be interpreted on a *drash* basis.

How does the *drash* deal with these points?

YOUR ANSWER:

UNDERSTANDING THE DRASH _____

An Answer: The *drash* interpretation deftly handles all of these points.

> * The terms "innocent" and "righteous" are interpreted in judicial terms. "Righteous" means one who was acquitted in court; "innocent" means one who is not guilty in reality, even if found guilty in court.
>
> * This verse speaks of judicial matters.
>
> * "Righteous" and "innocent" are not synonymous; the difference between them is significant.
>
> * The Sixth Commandment does not refer to the type of cases presented here and thus there is no unnecessary repetition here.
>
> (See *Be'er Yitzchak*)

Exodus 23:8

וְשֹׁחַד לֹא תִקָּח כִּי הַשֹּׁחַד יְעַוֵּר פִּקְחִים וִיסַלֵּף דִּבְרֵי צַדִּיקִים.

דברי צדיקים: דברים המצודקים. משפטי אמת, וכן תרגומו
פתגמין תריצים—ישרים.

Words of justice: *Rashi*: Words that are just, i.e., judg-
ments of truth. So too does the Targum [Onkelos] translate it: 'words that are—תריצים righteous'.

WHAT IS RASHI SAYING?

Rashi translates the words of the *dibbur hamaschil* דברי צדיקים as "words
of justice." This is as if the Hebrew were דברים צדיקים, where "righteous" is an adjective defining the noun "words." He does not take these
words to mean "the words of the righteous".

What would you ask here?

YOUR QUESTION:

QUESTIONING RASHI

A Question: Rashi's rendition is unexpected, since the words are דברי צדיקים
where the word דברי is in the construct state, meaning "words of..."
Thus the simplest translation of these words would be "the words
of the righteous." That is, "the words of the judges," parallel to the
first half of the verse where it says "the eyes of the wise."

Why does Rashi choose the less obvious meaning?

What's bothering him?

YOUR ANSWER:

WHAT IS BOTHERING RASHI?

An Answer: The Torah would not call a judge 'righteous' if he had accepted a
bribe. For this reason alone Rashi sought another meaning to these
words.

How does his interpretation avoid this problem?

YOUR ANSWER:

Understanding Rashi

An Answer: By taking a bribe, the judge distorts the 'righteous words' of the Torah. He rationalizes an illegal decision in order to justify taking the bribe. The grammatical problem—i.e., דברי being the construct state—can be overcome. There are exceptions to this rule. The most obvious example of such exceptions are the words מי המרים, "the bitter waters" (Numbers 5:23). The word מי apparently in the construct state (which would mean 'waters of bitterness') is, in fact, not so. It is used, rather, as an adjective describing the waters, just as, in our verse, the word דברי can be an adjective describing 'words.'

(See Nachlas Ya'akov)

פרשת תרומה

Exodus 25:2

דַּבֵּר אֶל בְּנֵי יִשְׂרָאֵל וְיִקְחוּ לִי תְּרוּמָה מֵאֵת כָּל אִישׁ אֲשֶׁר יִדְּבֶנּוּ
לִבּוֹ תִּקְחוּ אֶת תְּרוּמָתִי.

ויקחו לי תרומה: לי–לשמי.

That they take to Me an offering. *Rashi:* "To Me"—for
My sake.

What would you ask on this brief comment?

YOUR QUESTION:

QUESTIONING RASHI

A Question: The words וְיִקְחוּ לִי " That they take to Me" are problematic.

In what way(s) are they problematic?

YOUR ANSWER:

WHAT IS BOTHERING RASHI?

An Answer: The words are awkward. One doesn't "take to" rather one "gives
to" or "takes from." How can we understand the meaning of this
construction?

But in addition to this syntactical problem, there are several conceptual
difficulties with this verse.

One obvious problem is: How does anyone give something to G-d? Where
and in what way is the transfer made?

Another problem is: Why should anyone give anything to G-d, He is the
Creator of the universe, the Owner of all that exists? As King David
said, "To Him is the earth and the fullness thereof!" (Psalms 24:1) The

prophet Chagai said likewise, "To Me is the silver and the gold, says *Hashem,* the L-rd of the Hosts" (Chagai 2:8).

He lacks nothing and all belongs to Him.

How does Rashi's comment deal with this?

YOUR ANSWER:

UNDERSTANDING RASHI

An Answer: The contributions were not *given to* G-d, they were *taken* from one's possessions and given for the use of the Tabernacle, which was intended, not for G-d, but for G-d's sake, for His glory.

(See Mizrachi, Gur Aryeh)

A difficult comment that has kept the commentators busy. Solving the mystery requires detective work.

Exodus 25:2
Same verse as above.

תקחו **את תרומתי.** אמרו רבותינו שלוש תרומות אמורות כאן,
אחת תרומת בקע לגולגולת שנעשו מהם האדנים, כמו שמפורש
באלה פקודי, ואחת תרומת המזבח בקע לגולגולת לקופות לקנות
מהן קרבנות צבור, ואחת תרומת המשכן נדבת כל אחד ואחד.
י"ג דברים האמורים בענין כולם הוצרכו למלאכת המשכן או
לבגדי כהונה כשתדקדק בהם.

You shall take My offering. *Rashi:* Our Rabbis said: the word תרומה is used here three times, [alluding to three different offerings] one is the heave offering which consisted of a *bekka* per individual, that was used to make the sockets, as it says in *Pekudei*; another is the heave offering for the altar, a *bekka* per individual, for the fund from which were purchased the communal sacrifices; and one is a heave offering for the Tabernacle which was a free-will gift from the individual. The thirteen different materials mentioned in this section were all required either for the work of the Tabernacle or for the priests' garments, as you will see if you look closely into the matter.

WHAT IS RASHI SAYING? _____

Rashi states that the Israelites actually made three different contributions to the Tabernacle and the fund for animal sacrifices. This is derived from the fact that the word תרומה is repeated three times in verses 25:2–3. Two of these offerings were obligatory (per individual) while the one mentioned in our chapter was voluntary. Rashi then mentions that the thirteen materials mentioned in this section were used for the Tabernacle and the priests' garments. Our analysis will first focus on this latter comment.

What can you ask about this statement?

Hint:

Count the materials listed in verse 25:3–7.

YOUR QUESTION:

QUESTIONING RASHI _____

Let us count them. 1) Gold, 2) Silver, 3) Copper, 4) Blue purple wool, 5) Red purple wool, 6) Crimson wool, 7) Fine linen, 8) Goats' hair, 9) Red dyed rams' skins, 10) Tachash skins, 11) Acacia wood, 12) Oil for the light, 13) Spices for anointing oil and for incense, 14) Onyx stones, 15) Stones for the ephod and the breastplate.

The question is obvious: How does Rashi arrive at 13 when there are 15?

Can you suggest an answer:

YOUR ANSWER:

EXPLAINING RASHI _____

Several answers have been suggested.

1) There are only 13 *different* materials here since the wool was dyed in three different colors, blue, red and crimson. (*Mizrachi*)

2) Rashi is telling us the purpose of those materials whose purpose is *not* mentioned in these verses. Two of them, oil for light and stones for the ephod, are stated clearly. That leaves 13. (*Silbermann*)

But the intriguing part of Rashi's comment are his words "if you look closely into the matter." What does Rashi mean by this? Why the need to look closely? It would seem obvious that if we check the objects of the Tabernacle and the garments of the priests (which are described in *parshios Terumah* and *T'tzaveh*), we will find these thirteen materials used in their construction.

This has puzzled commentators.

It is a difficult question. Can you suggest an answer?

Hint:

Look at Rashi's next comment on verse 25:3.

YOUR ANSWER:

UNDERSTANDING RASHI

An Answer: In order to understand Rashi, we must remember that this phrase is part of his general comment on this (and the next) verse. This is generally a good rule to follow—understand Rashi's words in the context of his surrounding comments

What did Rashi say above? That there are three offerings תרומות; two are obligatory and one a voluntary contribution; the one mentioned in this section is the voluntary one.

In the next verse (25:3) Rashi says:

> **"Gold and silver and copper etc.** *Rashi:* All of these came voluntarily, from each individual as much as his heart moved him. *Except for the silver which came equally, a half-shekel* [obligatory] *from each one.* And we have not found in the whole construction of the Tabernacle that more silver [than the half-shekel] was needed, as it says "And the silver of those who were counted of the assembly, etc., a *bekka* per individual, etc. (Ch. 38:25-26)." The rest of the silver that came as a voluntary contribution was made into service vessels [for the Tabernacle].

WHAT IS RASHI SAYING?

Rashi tells us that every material in this list of 13 was donated voluntarily, except for the silver, which was obligatory. So we can ask: Why then is silver listed here, since Rashi had already said that *this* תרומה is a voluntary one. Rashi answers this himself when he says, at the end of the comment, "The rest of the silver that came as a voluntary contribution was made into service vessels."

But there is a problem with this statement.

If you read the *parshios* carefully, you can see the problem.

What is the problem?

What's bothering Rashi?

YOUR ANSWER:

WHAT IS BOTHERING RASHI? _____

An Answer: If you search the four *parshios* of *Terumah*, *T'tzaveh*, *Vayakhel* and *Pekudei*, you cannot find silver being used for anything else besides the sockets and the filings of the pillars. Verses 38:27-28 sums it up: "The hundred *kikar* silver were used to pour the sockets of the sanctity and the sockets of the *paroches* ... and for the hooks for the pillars and the coverings of their heads and their filings." All this silver came from the obligatory *bekka* per head. But Rashi had said "the rest was from voluntary contributions and it was used for vessels for the Tabernacle." Yet close inspection of these *parshios* shows that there are *no other silver objects*! So what was made from the voluntary contributions of silver?

This is what's bothering Rashi.

Can you solve the missing silver mystery?

YOUR ANSWER:

THE MYSTERY OF THE MISSING SILVER _____

An Answer: In order to answer this question, we have to look much further on in the Torah, in Numbers 10:2, where it says:
"Make for yourself two silver trumpets. You shall make them hammered from silver, and they shall be for you for summoning the assembly and for causing the camps to journey."

Here we find the use of the voluntary silver; it was used to make the trumpets, which were vessels for the Tabernacle. This is what Rashi had in mind when he wrote "if you look closely into the matter", since you have to search all the way to chapter 10 in the book of Numbers to find that additional, voluntary, silver was needed for the vessels of the Tabernacle!

A Lesson

Never gloss over any of Rashi's words. They all make sense when delved into. By now this should be a familiar message, one worth remembering.

(See Silbermann; *Yosef Hallel*)

Rashi asks his own question, an unusual event. But the Ramban isn't satisfied with the answer he gives.

Exodus 25:21

וְנָתַתָּ אֶת הַכַּפֹּרֶת עַל הָאָרֹן מִלְמָעְלָה וְאֶל הָאָרֹן תִּתֵּן אֶת הָעֵדֻת אֲשֶׁר אֶתֵּן אֵלֶיךָ.

ואל הארן תתן את העדות. לא ידעתי למה נכפל, שהרי כבר נאמר 'ונתת אל הארון את העדות'. ויש לומר שבא ללמד שבעודו ארון לבדו בלא כפורת, יתן תחלה העדות לתוכו ואחר כך יתן את הכפרת עליו. וכן מצינו כשהקים את המשכן נאמר 'ויתן את העדות אל הארון' ואחר כך 'ויתן את הכפורת על הארון מלמעלה.'

And into the Ark you shall place the Testimony. *Rashi:* I do not know why it is repeated, for it has already said: (above 25:16) "You shall place in the Ark the Testimony"? It may be answered that this comes to teach that when the Ark is alone, without the cover, he should first place the Testimony in it and only afterwards place the cover on it. So we do actually find when he [Moses] erected the Tabernacle, it states (Exodus 40:20): "He placed the Testimony in the Ark" and [only] afterwards, "He placed the cover on the Ark on the top."

An unusual Rashi-comment. Rashi asks his question openly, which he hardly ever does and then he suggests his answer.

Even though the comment is straightforward, and he, himself, tells us what's bothering him, nevertheless we can still question it.

Hint:

Look at the complete verse. How does it match up with Rashi's conclusion?

YOUR QUESTION:

QUESTIONING RASHI

A Question: The order of things as described in our verse is: First put the cover on the Ark, then put the Testimony inside. Rashi says just the opposite!

Why?

YOUR ANSWER:

If your answer is that verse 40:20 has the order in a way that supports Rashi, for it says, in effect, first place the Testimony in the Ark, then place the cover on it, we would ask: Why should that verse be any more authoritative than our verse which says the opposite?

Hint:

Look closely at the words in both verses.

YOUR ANSWER:

UNDERSTANDING RASHI

An Answer: Did you notice that our verse, in Hebrew, has the noun,'the Ark' before the verb, 'you shall place," while verse 25:16 has the verb, 'you shall place' before the noun, the Ark'? This is our clue. In biblical Hebrew, when the noun comes before the verb, the tense is the pluperfect, meaning that the action took place before the previously mentioned action. The classic example is found in Genesis 4:1, והאדם ידע את חוה אשתו, "And Adam knew Eve his wife." There Rashi teaches us this principle. Since "Adam" comes before "knew" the meaning is "he had already known," even *before* the previous event described (being evicted from the Garden of Eden).

See that our verse says: "And into *the Ark* (noun) you shall *place* (verb) the Testimony." The noun comes before the verb, meaning that this act (of placing the Testimony in the Ark) came *before* the previously mentioned action ("And place the cover on the Ark"). This is exactly as Rashi says. There is, therefore, no contradiction between the two verses.

This biblical grammatical rule, though not well known, can be crucial to a correct understanding of the Torah's meaning. See an obvious use of this rule in the case of Rachel's hiding her father's *teraphim* in Genesis 31:34. But an unusual and surprising implication of this rule can be found in Esau's sale of his birthright to Jacob. Look closely at Genesis 25:34 and you will arrive at a startling revelation. If you can't discover it yourself, see the *K'sav V'Hakabalah*. If all else fails, see my book *Studying the Torah*, pages 31–34.

THE RAMBAN DISAGREES WITH RASHI

After quoting Rashi, the Ramban writes:

"But if this is a command [as Rashi has it], the sense thereof would rather seem to be that after he puts the cover on the Ark as G-d had commanded, [he should then remove the cover] put the Testimony into the Ark, for the term 'Ark' applies also when there is a cover on it. Moreover, one can also ask why did Scripture repeat the phrase (verse 22) *"from between the two cherubim which are upon the Ark of the Testimony,"* when it is already known from the preceding verses that the cherubim are upon the Ark of Testimony? And what need is there to explain this again, seeing that He has already stated (verse 22), *from above the kapores (cover), from between the two cherubim*?

"But the explanation is as follows: Because He had commanded (verse 20) that *the cherubim shall spread out their wings on high* but had not said why they should be made altogether and what function they should serve in the Tabernacle and why they should be in that form, therefore He now said *and you shall put the cover* with the cherubim, for they are all one, *above the Ark*, because *in the Ark you shall put the Testimony that I shall give you*, so that there be for Me a Throne of Glory, for there will I meet with you and I will cause My Glory to dwell upon them *and I will speak with you from above the cover from between the two cherubim* because it is *upon the Ark of the Testimony.* It is thus identical with the Divine Chariot which the prophet Ezekiel saw, of which he said (Ezekiel 10:20), *This is the living creature that I saw under the G-d of Israel by the river Chebar, and I knew that they were cherubim.* This is why He (G-d) is called (Samuel I 4:4) "He who sits upon the cherubim" for they spread out their wings on high in order to teach us that they are the Chariot who carry the Glory..."

WHAT IS THE RAMBAN SAYING?

The Ramban disagrees with Rashi in that he does not see the words "and in the Ark you shall put the Testimony" as a directive to Moses telling him where to put the Testimony. Remember, Rashi had asked that these words were redundant since we were already told to put the Testimony in the Ark.

The Ramban has a very different view of all these verses. In view of the questions he poses (the apparent unnecessary repetitions), he believes all the redundancies here are meant to stress a particular point.

Which point is that?

YOUR ANSWER:

UNDERSTANDING THE RAMBAN

An Answer: The whole point here, says the Ramban, is to clarify the purpose of the cherubim. They are to be the throne for G-d's Glory. But these cherubim are meaningful only because they are part and parcel of the cover of the Ark which contains the words of G-d's Testimony (the Tablets with the Ten Commandments).

How does the Ramban's explanation answer the question that Rashi posed?

YOUR ANSWER:

An Answer: When we look at all these verses 17–22, we see that the making of the cherubim are discussed. They are placed on the Ark, to serve as its cover, and then the Torah emphasizes (by repetition) that *in this Ark is placed the Testimony.* The repetition of these words, which Rashi finds puzzling, the Ramban understands as being used for emphasis. This is the seat, so to speak, of G-d's Spirit, above the uplifted wings of the cherubim *which is above the Testimony.*

THE TABLETS OF TESTIMONY

Why are the Tablets on which were inscribed the Ten Commandments called the Tablets of Testimony לוחות העדות? Because they serve as witness to *Hashem's* communication to Israel at Sinai, and to the fact that He chose Israel to be His special representative in this world. Above the Testimony, therefore, is the most fitting place for G-d's presence to be situated and particularly suited to be the source of His communications to Israel. As it says (verse 22) "And I will speak to you from above the cover from between the cherubim that are on the Ark of the Testimony."

THE CHERUBIM

What were the Cherubim? They were two winged human figures with childlike faces (see Rashi 25:18). They were fashioned from gold and were standing, attached to the cover (*kapores*) of the Ark, their wings raised above their heads, pointing heavenward.

These were a most incongruous feature of the Tabernacle. These cherubim, which were graven images, were placed in the Holy of Holies, of all places, above the Ten Commandments, of all places. The third Commandment of the Tablets prohibits making any graven image and here perched on top of these Tablets were the images of the cherubim ! Strange, to say the least. Why?

The surest statement that can be made in this regard is that G-d commanded the making of these cherubim and to paraphrase Shakespeare "Nothing is good or bad but G-d's thinking makes it so." This incongruity between the graven image placed on top of the Commandment prohibiting the making of graven images, highlights the centrality of G-d's will in determining "right" and "wrong."

Likewise, we find illicit sexual alliances become sanctioned when following Divine will, see the relationship of Tamar and her father-in-law Judah (Genesis, ch. 38). Their union eventually produced a King David. Even impassioned killing becomes sanctioned when in accordance with the Divine will. Pinchas' brazen and grotesque killing of Zimri and Cozbi (Numbers 25:11-15) led to a Covenant of Peace.

And graven images not only become sanctioned but are given an honored place in the Holy of Holies, when such is the Divine will.

(See *Ibn Ezra*)

Get out your calculator and see if you can understand this Rashi-comment.

Exodus 27:9-10

וְעָשִׂיתָ אֵת חֲצַר הַמִּשְׁכָּן לִפְאַת נֶגֶב תֵּימָנָה קְלָעִים לֶחָצֵר שֵׁשׁ מָשְׁזָר מֵאָה בָאַמָּה אֹרֶךְ לַפֵּאָה הָאֶחָת. וְעַמֻּדָיו עֶשְׂרִים וְאַדְנֵיהֶם עֶשְׂרִים נְחֹשֶׁת וָוֵי הָעַמֻּדִים וַחֲשֻׁקֵיהֶם כָּסֶף.

וְעַמֻּדָיו עֶשְׂרִים. חמש אמות בין עמוד לעמוד.

And twenty columns thereof. *Rashi* : [There was a space of] five cubits between one column and the other.

WHAT IS RASHI SAYING?

The courtyard of the Tabernacle was 100 cubits long and 50 cubits wide. The length (North and South sides) had 20 columns. Rashi tells us that between each column there was a space of 5 cubits.

What would you ask on this comment?

Hint:

Do a little arithmetic.

YOUR QUESTION:

QUESTIONING RASHI

A Question: Twenty columns means there were nineteen spaces between them. If each space was five cubits, then $19 \times 5 = 95$. But the length was 100 cubits?!

How can this be?

YOUR ANSWER:

UNDERSTANDING RASHI

Several solutions have been suggested to this problem.

The *Abarbanel* says the width of the columns was not included in the sum total. So when we add them to 95 cubits we arrive at 100 cubits. Each column was 1 and $1/4$ *tephachim* (handbreadths) in width. Each cubit is made up of 5 *tephachim*. Therefore 20 (columns) × 1 ¹/4 = 25 *tephachim*; 25 ÷ 5 = 5 additional cubits. See Diagram A, page 162.

The *Mizrachi,* on the other hand, says that the width of the columns was included in the 5 cubits. He offers a very reasonable solution. The North and South sides each had 20 columns, the East and West sides each had 10 columns. Now the North side, for example, in actuality had 21 columns, because the North-East corner's column was the tenth column of the East-side, thus it was in both the East-side row of columns and the North-side row of columns. See Diagram B, page 163.

The solution is perfect...until we come to another Rashi comment a few verses further.

Caution! The following analysis requires clear-headed thinking.

Exodus 27:14

וַחֲמֵשׁ עֶשְׂרֵה אַמָּה קְלָעִים לַכָּתֵף עַמֻּדֵיהֶם שְׁלֹשָׁה וְאַדְנֵיהֶם שְׁלֹשָׁה.

עמדיהם שלשה. חמש אמות בין עמוד לעמוד, בין עמוד שבראש הדרום העומד במקצוע דרומית מזרחית עד עמוד שהוא מן השלשה שבמזרח חמש אמות וממנו לשני חמש אמות, ומן השני לשלישי חמש אמות, וכן לכתף השנית, וארבעה עמודים למסך, הרי עשרה עמודים למזרח כנגד עשרה למערב.

Their columns, three. *Rashi:* There were five cubits between one column and the next column; between the column at the end of the southern row, standing at the South-east corner, to the [first] column which was one of the three in the East there were five cubits, from that to the second, five cubits, and from the second to the third, five cubits. It was similar at the other side [of the entrance]. And four columns for the screen [of the entrance], so you have ten columns for the East side corresponding to the ten columns in the West side.

What Is Rashi Saying?

Rashi is explaining the different arrangement of columns (and spaces) on the East side of the Tabernacle courtyard. On this side was the entrance into the courtyard. The entrance was an opening space of 20 cubits between the curtains and the columns on its right side (North) and its left side (South). On these two sides were 15 cubits each; that together with the 20 cubits of the entrance, equalled the 50 cubits on the

East side. The entrance was protected by the *masach,* screen, which was set back 10 *tephachim* from the entrance to allow entrance from either side.

THE PROBLEM

Can you see a problem here?

There is a big one!

What is it?

> *Hint:*
>
> Take some lego blocks and place them as columns in formation as the courtyard. The main problem is the East side with the *masach.* To follow Rashi's conditions you must fulfill the following requirements:
> * Equal space on the N and S sides of the *masach*, with three columns each.
> * The *masach* itself having four columns.
> * There must be 5 cubits from the SE column to the first column on the East side.

YOUR ANSWER:

This is really a puzzle. There does not seem to be any way to work this out.

To show how difficult this is, look at the diagrams in the *Artscroll Chumash* and in the *Metsudah Chumash/Rashi.*

Artscroll shows the *masach* without drawing the columns. Apparently they couldn't figure out how to illustrate them!

Metsudah does show the *masach* and its columns, but it is flush with the N and S sides. That can't be, because then there is no way to enter the courtyard! But more problematic is that the diagram pictures 12 columns on the East side which translates into 55 cubits (5 cubits per space between columns); but the side is supposed to have only 50 cubits!

Both have sidestepped this difficult Rashi.

Let us look closer at the solutions offered by the Abarbanel and the *Mizrachi.* The accompanying diagrams should help. *Don't be frightened by the arithmetic, it is not really difficult. Take it slow, so you can understand what all the fuss is about. Maybe you can offer a better solution.*

SOME SUGGESTED SOLUTIONS

See diagrams A and B, the Abarbanel's and *Mizrachi*'s solutions, and their difficulties.

Diagram A — Abarbanel's solution

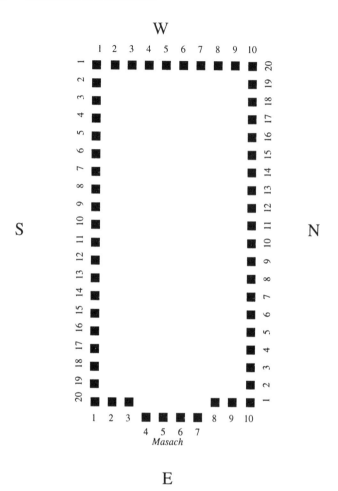

The problem: Here there is a problem with the East and West sides. For the columns to make up the slack in the 5 cubits, we need them to be 1 ¹/4 *tephachim* for the long sides, as we explained above. But for the shorter East and West sides, these columns would have to be twice that size, i.e., 3 *tephachim* each. The *Mizrachi* criticizes this solution for this reason, i.e., it would be very odd-looking if the columns surrounding the tabernacle were of different, non-uniform sizes.

Diagram B — the *Mizrachi*'s solution

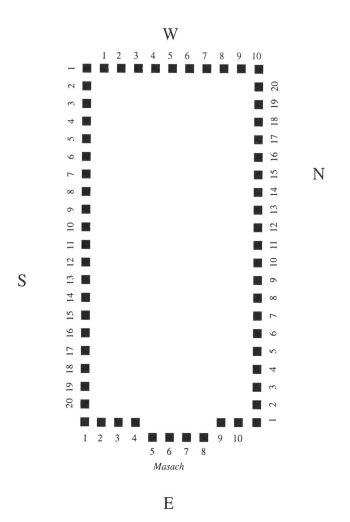

The problem: The East side does not coincide with Rashi's point (27:14) that the columns and spaces on one side of the *masach* were similar to those on the other side. In this diagram, there are four on one side and three on the other!

Do you have a solution?

YOUR ANSWER:

A POSSIBLE SOLUTION _____

See theAppendix (page 205) for a possible solution to this difficult Rashi.

Rashi gently guides us away from a misunderstanding.

Exodus 27:21

בְּאֹהֶל מוֹעֵד מִחוּץ לַפָּרֹכֶת אֲשֶׁר עַל הָעֵדֻת יַעֲרֹךְ אֹתוֹ אַהֲרֹן וּבָנָיו מֵעֶרֶב עַד בֹּקֶר לִפְנֵי הי חֻקַּת עוֹלָם לְדֹרֹתָם מֵאֵת בְּנֵי יִשְׂרָאֵל.

מערב עד בקר: תֵּן לָה מִדָּתָה שֶׁתְּהֵא דּוֹלֶקֶת מֵעֶרֶב עַד בֹּקֶר. וְשִׁיעֲרוּ חֲכָמִים חֲצִי לוֹג לְלֵילֵי טֵבֵת הָאֲרוּכִים וְכֵן לְכָל הַלֵּילוֹת וְאִם יוֹתֵר אֵין בְּכָךְ כְּלוּם.

From evening to morning. *Rashi:* Give it its due measure so that it will burn from evening to morning. Our Sages estimated a half *log* [sufficient] for the nights of Teveth which are long, and [the same] for every night, and if any were left over it did not matter.

The first part of Rashi's statement seems to be a Type II comment. Notice how he just adds a few words ("Give it its due measure so it will burn") which he inserts them into the Torah text ("from evening to morning"). This means that his comment is meant to steer us clear of a possible misunderstanding.

Which misunderstanding?

Hint:

Read the whole verse.

YOUR ANSWER:

A Possible Misunderstanding

An Answer: The verse says "Aaron and his sons shall arrange it from evening until morning, etc." Does this mean they should spend the whole night, *from evening until morning,* arranging the lights?

Certainly not!

This is the misunderstanding that Rashi is addressing.

How does his comment deal with this?

YOUR ANSWER:

UNDERSTANDING RASHI

An Answer: Rashi alerts us to the fact that the Hebrew word יַעֲרֹךְ in our verse has two possible meanings. It can mean either "to arrange" as in שולחן ערוך "an arranged table." Or it can mean "to estimate" as in "the priest shall *estimate its value* whether it is good or bad; as the priest *estimates its value* יַעֲרִיךְ אוֹתוֹ so shall it be established. (Leviticus 27:14)"

Rashi has chosen the second meaning, "to estimate." He says "give it its due measure so that it will burn from evening until morning. The Sages estimated, etc." In this way Rashi deftly avoids the misunderstanding. The priests do not *arrange it* from evening until morning, rather they *estimate* how much oil is necessary to burn from evening until morning.

A LESSON

At first glance, this Rashi-comment seems to be strictly informative, telling us how much oil was used in the candelabrum. But sensitivity to Rashi's style makes us aware that Rashi never *just* informs. When we search, we find that his comment is meant to clarify something about the Torah's words themselves.

(See *LiPhshuto shel Rashi*)

Exodus 28:3

וְאַתָּה תְּדַבֵּר אֶל כָּל חַכְמֵי לֵב אֲשֶׁר מִלֵּאתִיו רוּחַ חָכְמָה וְעָשׂוּ אֶת
בִּגְדֵי אַהֲרֹן לְקַדְּשׁוֹ לְכַהֲנוֹ לִי.

לְקַדְּשׁוֹ לְכַהֲנוֹ לִי. לקדשו להכניסו בכהונה על ידי הבגדים שיהא
כהן לי ולשון כהונה שירות הוא.

To sanctify him to make him a priest for Me. *Rashi*: To
sanctify him, i.e., to install him into the priesthood by
means of the garments, so that he may become a priest
for Me. The expression of כהונה means to serve—
serventrice in Old French.

WHAT IS RASHING SAYING?

Rashi here is attempting to clarify the words in the *dibbur hamaschil* for
us. He uses different phrases to say apparently the same thing. He says
"to install into the priesthood," and "so that he may become a priest for
Me," and finally "כהונה means to serve." Why does he do this?

What is bothering him?

YOUR ANSWER:

An Initial Analysis

The meaning of the words לכהנו לי is unclear. There are several possible
translations of these words, all have difficulties. Let us compare them.
In our analysis we include the word לקדשו, "to sanctify him", because
Rashi does, even though all three versions translate it the same. Rashi
includes this word in his *dibbur hamaschil,* he also begins his comment
with this word, so it is related to his comment.

1) לקדשו	2) לקדשו	3) לקדשו
"to sanctify him"	"to sanctify him"	"to sanctify him"
לכהנו	לכהנו	לכהנו
"for him to serve"	"to make him a priest"	"for his becoming a priest"
לי	לי	לי
"Me"	"for Me"	"for Me"

Pay close attention to the differences between them. Now we will look
at each one:

WHAT IS BOTHERING RASHI?

An Answer:

Option No. 1 has a problem with the word לי. If we say "to serve", then the Hebrew should be אותי and not לי. Nevertheless, this is the way *Onkelos* translates it.

Option No. 2 has a problem because the meaning is that two acts are taking place here: 1. "to sanctify him", and 2. "to make him a priest." Therefore there should be a connecting ו between the two: "to sanctify him **and** to make him a priest." Since the ו is absent, this weakens this option.

Option No. 3 appears to be problem-free; it would seem to be the one that Rashi chooses.

How do Rashi's words clarify matters?

YOUR ANSWER:

UNDERSTANDING RASHI

An Answer: Rashi is telling us that the word לכהנו is intended to explain the word לקדשו. The priest becomes "sanctified" by means of wearing the priestly garments; wearing them the first time has the effect of causing him to enter the priesthood. These words show us that the words " for his becoming a priest" are intended to explain what is meant by "to sanctify him". That is why there is no connecting "and" here. Rashi continues with "so he may become a priest for Me", to explain the words לכהנו לי. They don't mean "to serve", they mean "for his becoming a priest."

A CLOSER LOOK

Did you notice that the words לכהנו לי already appear in an earlier verse (28:1)? There it says:

וְאַתָּה הַקְרֵב אֵלֶיךָ אֶת אַהֲרֹן אָחִיךָ וְאֶת בָּנָיו אִתּוֹ מִתּוֹךְ בְּנֵי יִשְׂרָאֵל
לְכַהֲנוֹ לִי אַהֲרֹן נָדָב וַאֲבִיהוּא אֶלְעָזָר וְאִיתָמָר בְּנֵי אַהֲרֹן.

Why didn't Rashi deal with them there?

A tough question. Are you up to it?

Hint:

Compare Options No. 1, No. 2, and No. 3. Which one of them best fits the meaning in verse 28:1?

YOUR ANSWER:

A Deeper Understanding

An Answer: It seems that in verse 28:1 all options are possible. In this verse these words could mean "for him to serve Me", or "to make him a priest for Me", or "for his becoming a priest for Me." Only when we get to our verse with the previous word, לקדשו, can we be sure that only Option No. 3 is appropriate, because there is no connecting ו. It is for this reason that Rashi waited until our verse to explain the words לכהנו לי. This also explains why Rashi included the word לקדשו in his *dibbur hamaschil*, and used it as the first word in this comment, because this word helps us understand the correct meaning of the words לכהנו לי.

A Remaining Problem

One problem does remain with this interpretation, it is with his last words. He says that "the word כהונה means 'service.' " It is hard to square this with his saying that לכהנו here means "for his becoming a priest" and not "for him to serve."

(See Silbermann, *LiPhshuto shel Rashi*)

This is a Rashi original. A unique interpretation for which no source can be found.

Exodus 28:30

וְנָתַתָּ אֶל חֹשֶׁן הַמִּשְׁפָּט אֶת הָאוּרִים וְאֶת הַתֻּמִּים וְהָיוּ עַל לֵב אַהֲרֹן בְּבֹאוֹ לִפְנֵי הי וְנָשָׂא אַהֲרֹן אֶת מִשְׁפַּט בְּנֵי יִשְׂרָאֵל עַל לִבּוֹ לִפְנֵי הי תָּמִיד.

אֶת הָאוּרִים וְאֶת הַתֻּמִּים. הוּא כְּתָב שֵׁם הַמְּפֹרָשׁ שֶׁהָיָה נוֹתְנוֹ בְּתוֹךְ כִּפְלֵי הַחֹשֶׁן שֶׁעַל יָדוֹ הוּא מֵאִיר דְּבָרָיו וּמְתַמֵּם אֶת דְּבָרָיו. וּבְמִּקְדָּשׁ שֵׁנִי הָיָה הַחֹשֶׁן שֶׁאִי אֶפְשָׁר לְכֹהֵן גָּדוֹל לִהְיוֹת מְחוּסַּר בְּגָדִים–אֲבָל אוֹתוֹ הַשֵּׁם לֹא הָיָה בְּתוֹכוֹ, וְעַל שֵׁם אוֹתוֹ הַכְּתָב הוּא קָרוּי מִשְׁפָּט, שֶׁנֶּאֱמַר 'וְשָׁאַל לוֹ בְּמִשְׁפַּט הָאוּרִים' (במדבר 27:21).

The Urim and Tumim. *Rashi:* This is the inscription of the Proper Name [of *Hashem*] which was placed between the folds of the breastplate through which its words were made clear (מאיר) and made perfectly true (ומתמם). In the second Temple there was a breastplate, because the High Priest cannot lack any of the [priestly] garments, but the Divine Name was not inside it. It was on account of this inscription that [the breastplate] was called "judgement" as it said "and he shall ask of the judgement of the Urim (Numbers 27:21)."

The fact that the Urim and the Tumim were identified with the Proper Name of *Hashem* is a statement made by Rashi for which no source can be found! It appears to be an idea that Rashi discovered on his own. The

THE RAMBAN SUPPORTS RASHI

Ramban agrees with Rashi on this and offers several indications that his suggestion is correct. He writes at length here. I will quote a large, but only partial, selection from his comment:

"It was this reason that the breastplate had to be double [so the Urim could be placed inside the fold]. The proof for this is that in the work of the craftsmen, the Urim and the Tumim are not mentioned at all, neither in the command nor in the [description of the] making of it. Now concerning the garments He details 'And he made the ephod and he made the breastplate' (39:8) but it does not say 'and he made the Urim and the Tumim.' And if it were the work of a skilled engraver, He would have dealt with it in greater length than with all [the garments]. Even if perhaps He desired to shorten the discussion about them on account of their profundity, He would at least have said here, 'and you shall make the Urim and the Tumim as it has been shown to you in the mount; of pure gold — or pure silver — you shall make them.' Moreover you will notice that He did not use the definite article (ה' הידיעה) in connection with any of the vessels which had not been previously mentioned. Instead He said 'and they shall make *an* ark' (25:10); 'and you shall make *a* table' (25:23); 'and you shall make *a* candelabrum' (25:31). In the case of the Tabernacle, however, He said 'And you shall make *the* Tabernacle' (26:1) because He had already mentioned it: 'and let them make Me a Sanctuary' (25:8).

"Now with reference to the Urim and the Tumim He said 'and you shall put in the breastplate of judgement *the* Urim and *the* Tumim.' He had not [previously] commanded him to make them, yet Scripture mentions them with the definite article!

"Moreover Scripture mentions them with reference to Moses only, saying by way of command 'you shall put in the breastplate of judgement'; similarly, at the time of making them it says 'and in the breastplate he put the Urim and the Tumim' since they were not the work of craftsmen. Neither craftsmen nor the congregation of Israel had any part whatsoever in their making or in their donation, for they were a secret transmitted by the Almighty to Moses, he wrote them in holiness.

"They were thus of heavenly origin and therefore they are referred to without any specification and with the definite article.... Thus the Urim and the Tumim were holy Names of G-d and it was by virtue of the power residing in the Names that the letters inscribed upon the stones of the breastplate would light up before the eyes of the priest who inquired of their judgement...."

STYLES OF INTERPRETATION

The Ramban continues with a lengthy discussion of the use of the Urim and Tumim. Notice the different styles of Rashi and the Ramban in their commentary here.

See how brief Rashi is, even though this was his own idea and it is certainly a very profound matter. Notice, on the other hand, how the Ramban elaborates with both detailed proofs and extensive discussion regarding the use of the Urim. Each commentator relates to the very profound and mysterious matter of the Urim and Tumim in their own characteristic way of interpretation.

A Type II Rashi-comment, meant to clarify matters. Ramban brings some difficult arguments against him.

Exodus 28: 33-34

וְעָשִׂיתָ עַל שׁוּלָיו רִמֹּנֵי תְּכֵלֶת וְאַרְגָּמָן וְתוֹלַעַת שָׁנִי עַל שׁוּלָיו סָבִיב וּפַעֲמֹנֵי זָהָב בְּתוֹכָם סָבִיב.

פַּעֲמֹן זָהָב וְרִמּוֹן פַּעֲמֹן זָהָב וְרִמּוֹן עַל שׁוּלֵי הַמְּעִיל סָבִיב.

33. וּפַעֲמֹנֵי זהב: זגין עם ענבלין שבתוכם. **בתוכם סביב:** ביניהם סביב – בין שני רימונים, פעמון אחד דבוק ותלוי בשולי המעיל.

34. פעמן זהב ורמון פעמן זהב ורמון: אצלו.

33. And bells of gold. *Rashi*: Bells together with the clappers in them.

In the midst of them round about. *Rashi*: Between them, all the way around — between every two pomegranates there was one bell attached, and hanging from the hem of the robe.

34. A golden bell and pomegranate, a golden bell and pomegranate. *Rashi*: Next to it.

WHAT IS RASHI SAYING?

This is a typical Type II comment, i.e., Rashi inserts several of his own words into the Torah's words in order to clarify its meaning. The first comment ("And bells of gold") tells us the meaning of bells, viz. that thay have "sound blasting" clappers within the outer bells. The second comment ("In the midst, all around") clarifies that the bells were between the pomegranates all the way around the bottom of the robe. The third comment ("A golden pomegranate, etc") reinforces the second comment by reiterating that the pomegranates were next to the bells.

A Type II comment is meant to help us avoid a misunderstanding. What misunderstanding?

YOUR ANSWER:

WHAT MISUNDERSTANDING?

An Answer: I might have thought that the bells were *within* the pomegranates. See the Rashi above (28:33) where he says that the pomegranates were hollow. Perhaps the word בתוכם means "inside them", inside the pomegranates. Rashi therefore clarifies the meaning of the word. It means "between" and not "within."

A CLOSER LOOK AT RASHI'S WORDS

Look again at Rashi (verse 34) and see his words, "there was one bell attached, hanging, from the hem of the robe." What do these words add to our understanding?

YOUR ANSWER:

An Answer: Again Rashi clarifies matters. If the bells were *within* the pomegranates, then only the pomegranates would have been attached to the robe's hem. But, if as Rashi wants us to understand, the bells were not within but *next to* the pomegranates, then they too were sewn, attached and hanging from the hem.

THE RAMBAN'S VIEW

The Ramban takes the opposite approach. He writes in the middle of his comment to Exodus 28:31:

"I do not know either why the Rav (Rashi) made the bells independent objects, stating that there was one bell between every two pomegranates. For if so, the pomegranates served no purpose. If they were made just for the ornamentation, why were they made like hollow pomegranates? Let him make them rather like golden apples! Moreover, the Torah should have explained with what the bells should be hung, and whether hooks should be made on which to hang the bells. Instead [we must say] the bells were inside the pomegranates themselves, for the pomegranates were hollow and made in the shape of small pomegranates that have not yet burst open. And the bells were hidden inside, but visible through them...."

The Ramban finds support for his view later on in *parashas Pekudei* (Exodus 39:24-26).

There it says:

24.וַיַּעֲשׂוּ עַל שׁוּלֵי הַמְּעִיל רִמּוֹנֵי תְּכֵלֶת וְאַרְגָּמָן וְתוֹלַעַת שָׁנִי מָשְׁזָר.

25.וַיַּעֲשׂוּ פַעֲמֹנֵי זָהָב טָהוֹר וַיִּתְּנוּ אֶת הַפַּעֲמֹנִים בְּתוֹךְ הָרִמֹּנִים עַל שׁוּלֵי הַמְּעִיל סָבִיב בְּתוֹךְ הָרִמֹּנִים.

26. פַּעֲמֹן וְרִמֹּן פַּעֲמֹן וְרִמֹּן עַל שׁוּלֵי הַמְּעִיל סָבִיב לְשָׁרֵת כַּאֲשֶׁר צִוָּה ה' אֶת מֹשֶׁה.

24. And they made upon the hems of the robe pomegranates of blue purple and red purple and crimson and twined [linen].

25. And they made bells of pure gold and put the bells בתוך the pomegranates upon the hems of the robe around, בתוך, the pomegranates.

26. A bell and a pomegranate, a bell and a pomegranate, round about the hems of the robe to minister; as *Hashem* had commanded Moses.

Why, asks the Ramban, are the words "בתוך הרמונים" repeated twice in sentence 25? This special emphasis, he concludes, is further evidence that the bells were inside and not between the pomegranates.

Support for the Ramban's View

Can you find other evidence from these verses that support the Ramban?

> *Hint*:
>
> Look at our verses and the purpose for having the bells and the pomegranates.

Your Answer:

Some Answers:

> I would suggest two additional pieces of evidence to support the Ramban's view:
>
> #1: Note that sentence 24 only tells us that the pomegranates were attached to the hem of the robe. Sentence 25, which speaks of the bells, doesn't mention them being attached [directly] to the robe, only that they were בתוך the pomegranates, which were, themselves, attached to the robe.
>
> #2: Note also that verse 26 twice mentions "a bell and a pomegranate, a bell and a pomegranate." This sounds like "a bell and a pomegranate" were one unit, that is, that the bell was inside the pomegranate. Otherwise, if the Torah just wanted to impress upon us the fact that they were alternating, it could have written "a bell and a pomegranate and a bell."
>
> All these nuances point to the validity of the Ramban's view.

SUPPORT FOR RASHI'S VIEW

Can you find support for Rashi's view?

> *Hint:*
>
> Read these verses again and find the purpose of the bells and pomegranates.

YOUR ANSWER:

An Answer: If the whole point of having bells was, as it states: "and its sound shall be heard when he comes into the holy place .... (verse 35), " the bell would certainly be heard better if were not encapsulated within the woolen pomegranate ornaments.

As we see, both views can find support in the Torah-text. In this case we certainly will have to wait for Elijah the prophet to come. The Talmud often says, in cases of doubt, that the matter must await the coming of Elijah to clarify it. In his days, the Temple will be rebuilt, then we will be able to see the High Priest in his garments including his robe. Then we will know for certain whose view was right, that of Rashi or that of the Ramban!

(See *Mizrachi*)

In this comment Rashi provides p'shat and Ramban adds a deeper dimension.

Exodus 31:2

רְאֵה קָרָאתִי בְשֵׁם בְּצַלְאֵל בֶּן אוּרִי בֶן חוּר לְמַטֵּה יְהוּדָה.

קָרָאתִי בְשֵׁם. לעשות מלאכתי, את **בְּצַלְאֵל.**

I have called by name. *Rashi*: To accomplish My work, **Bezalel**.

A short comment. What would you ask?

YOUR QUESTION:

QUESTIONING RASHI

A Question: Rashi doesn't seem to add anything to what the Torah itself says. What purpose does this comment serve?

     Hint:

     What type of Rashi-comment is this?

YOUR ANSWER:

Answer: Notice Rashi's style here, it is short, he just inserts a few words into the Torah's words. This is characteristic of a Type II comment. What is the purpose of Type II comments?

YOUR ANSWER:

Answer: This type of comment is not meant to answer a difficulty in the text. Thus our usual question, *"What's bothering Rashi?"*, is not appropriate. This type of comment is rather meant to help us avoid a misunderstanding.

Which misunderstanding is possible here?

YOUR ANSWER:

WHICH MISUNDERSTANDING IS RASHI HELPING US AVOID? _____

An Answer: The words "I have called, by name, Bezalel..." can be understood in several ways.
1) I have called [his name] Bezalel
2) I have called: "Bezalel!"
3) I have called upon Bezalel

Which is the appropriate one here? Which does Rashi choose?

YOUR ANSWER:

UNDERSTANDING RASHI _____

An Answer: Rashi tells us that #3 is the correct reading. G-d is calling by name, that is, designating, Bezalel to do the work of the Tabernacle.

The misunderstanding is to think that the verse might mean that G-d called his name "Bezalel." Not really so strange, since we know that G-d does give certain special individuals a new name midway in their life. Abraham and Israel (Jacob) are two familiar examples.

Nevertheless, Rashi tells us this is not the meaning. How does he tell us this?

YOUR ANSWER:

An Answer: By adding the word את before the word "Bezalel" Rashi tells us that Bezalel is the direct object of the words "I have called." If the meaning were "I have called his name 'Bezalel' "(choice #1) then the direct object would be "his name" and the word את would be placed before it, קראתי **את** שמו בצלאל. If the meaning were "I have called: 'Bezalel' "(choice # 2) then there would be no את, it would read: קראתי בצלאל. By adding the word את before "Bezalel" Rashi eliminates possibility #2.

How does Rashi know that this is the correct meaning?

YOUR ANSWER:

Support for Rashi's Interpretation _____

An Answer: Nowhere in the Torah do we find G-d speaking to Bezalel directly. So choice #2, where G-d calls out directly to Bezalel, doesn't seem likely. Nor does it seem reasonable that G-d gave him a new name (choice #1). When G-d gives a new name to a person, the Torah offers an explanation for the change and tells us the meaning of the new name. Not so here.

The wording in this verse is unusual. It says "I have called *by name*, Bezalel..." What is the point of the words, "by name"? These mean "to designate," to choose one from among many.

Rashi also adds the words לעשות מלאכתי "to do My work."

Why does he do this?

YOUR ANSWER:

An Answer: Rashi has said that the meaning of קראתי בשם is "to designate", but the verse does not tell us what Bezalel was designated for. By adding "I have called ...*to do My work*", Rashi clarifies the purpose of this designation. While the immediate verses do not tell the purpose of the designation, the end of verse 31:5 does. There it says "to do all the work." Rashi has paraphrased this when he adds "to do My work."

Ramban's Interesting Insight _____

The Ramban offers an interesting insight at this point. He explains the significance of the special designation of Bezalel. Following are his words:

> "The reason for this [the special designation of Bezalel] is because Israel in Egypt had been crushed under the work "in mortar and in brick" and had acquired no knowledge of how to work with silver and gold and the cutting of precious stones and had never seen them at all. It was thus a wonder that there was to be found amongst them such a wise-hearted man who knew how to work with silver and gold and in cutting the stones [for setting] and in carving wood, a craftsman, an embroiderer and a weaver. For even amongst those who study before experts, you cannot find one who is proficient in all these crafts. And even those who know them and are used to

doing them, if their hands are continually engaged in [work with] lime and mud, they lose their ability to use them for such artistic and delicate work.... Therefore, G-d says to Moses that when he sees this wonder he should know that 'I filled him with the spirit of G-d' (verse 31:3) to know all these things in order that he would make the Tabernacle. "

Ramban adds dimension and depth to the words of the Torah. Bezalel is a real person with real experiences, some traumatic. He spent his whole life before the Exodus as a slave in Pharaoh's House of Bondage. When you add this to our understanding, we begin to grasp the giant step Bezalel had to take to become the Chief Artisan in the construction of the Tabernacle. This, then, is the deeper meaning of "I have called by name, Bezalel....and *I have filled him with the spirit of G-d...*" By designating Bezalel, G-d inspired this recently freed slave with the uncanny, literally G-d given talents to build the House of G-d in the wilderness.

(See *Mesiach Ilmim*)

The Ramban points out a serious difficulty with Rashi's interpretation.

Exodus 31:13

וְאַתָּה דַּבֵּר אֶל בְּנֵי יִשְׂרָאֵל לֵאמֹר אַךְ אֶת שַׁבְּתֹתַי תִּשְׁמֹרוּ כִּי אוֹת הוּא בֵּינִי וּבֵינֵיכֶם לְדֹרֹתֵיכֶם לָדַעַת כִּי אֲנִי הי מְקַדִּשְׁכֶם.

אַךְ אֶת שַׁבְּתֹתַי תִּשְׁמֹרוּ. אַף עַל פִּי שֶׁתִּהְיוּ רְדוּפִין וּזְרִיזִין בִּזְרִיזוּת הַמְלָאכָה, שַׁבָּת לֹא תִדָּחֶה מִפָּנֶיהָ. כָּל אַכִין וְרַקִּין מִעוּטִין—לְמַעֵט שַׁבָּת מִמְּלֶאכֶת הַמִּשְׁכָּן.

But My Sabbaths you shall keep. *Rashi:* Even though you will be anxious and alert to do the work promptly, you must not set aside the Sabbath on its account. The words אך and רק have a limiting effect. Here it is meant to exempt the Sabbath from [continuing] the work of the Tabernacle.

WHAT IS RASHI SAYING?

Rashi applies a Talmudic principle ("The words אך and רק have a limiting effect") to our verse. Since it says "But (אך) My Sabbaths..." it implies that the work of the Tabernacle, which is discussed immediately before this, is limited, i.e., it must not be done on the Sabbath.

RAMBAN'S CRITICISM OF RASHI

This Rashi-comment has caused quite a stir among the commentaries. The Ramban leads the attack. After quoting Rashi, the Ramban states the difficulty clearly. He writes:

"This is not correct in my opinion, because according to the *midrash* of our Rabbis the words, אך and רק would limit the observance of the Sabbath [and not limit the work of the Tabernacle]. Because the limitations in every place limit the matter that is being commanded. [In this case the Sabbath is being commanded, so *it* would be restricted.] Therefore, if you apply the limitation in the matter of constructing the Tabernacle, it would be *permissable* to construct it on the Sabbath."

WHAT IS THE RAMBAN SAYING?

This is a telling blow. The Ramban claims that Rashi is misinterpreting the Talmudic principle, that the words אך and רק always have a limiting force. The limitation, says the Ramban, is always of the *mitzvah* being commanded, that is, the word אך always limits the words that come *after* it, not before it. If it were, in fact, applied in our verse, then we would have to limit the command to rest on the Sabbath in deference to the command to construct the Tabernacle. Meaning, we should *not* rest on the Sabbath while the Tabernacle is being constructed, we should rather continue building it even on the Sabbath. But this is the opposite of the conclusion that Rashi draws.

The Ramban also points out that the Sages do, in fact, interpret these very same words, אך את שבתתי תשמרו, to limit the Sabbath. From these words, the Sages taught that life-saving behaviors (*pikuach nefesh*) or circumcision on the eight day can be performed on the Sabbath even though they entail violating the Day of Rest.

ATTEMPTS TO DEFEND RASHI

Many commentators come to Rashi's defense, the *Mizrachi* and, the *Gur Aryeh* among the foremost. One commentary, the *Tzedah Laderech*, goes so far as to claim that this is a misprint in Rashi; he never could have written such a thing. He suggests deleting these words from Rashi's commentary. While this solution is appealing and would neatly resolve this problem, it is not satisfactory. The Ramban was among the first commentators to comment on Rashi's commentary, about 130 years after Rashi's time. If the Ramban did have these words in his Rashi edition (more accurately, his "scroll"), then that would appear to be more authentic then the *Tzedah Laderech*'s speculation suggested hundreds of years later.

UNDERSTANDING RASHI

It is difficult to accept that Rashi misunderstood such a basic principle of אכין ורקין as the Ramban claims. Let us analyze the matter and see if we can understand what Rashi meant. We will look at several examples of the use of אך in the Torah to see if there is any pattern to them.

1) Genesis 9:(3). "Every creeping thing that lives shall be food for you, as the green herb have I given you all these things. (4). **Nevertheless** (אך) flesh with a soul thereof and the blood thereof you shall not eat. (5). **However** (אך) your own blood of your souls will I require, at the hand of every living soul will I require it."

Rashi comments on Verse 5:

"Although I have permitted you to take the life of cattle, **however** your blood I will surely require from him who sheds his own blood."

2) Numbers 1:44...49. "These are the numbered which Moses and Aaron numbered and the princes of Israel, twelve men, each one of the house of his fathers. ....(49) **But** (אך) the tribe of Levi you shall not number and their sum do not take among the Children of Israel."

Rashi comments here:

"The legion of the King (tribe of Levi) is worthy to be by itself." (Rashi gives us the reason why Levi was counted separately and not with all the other tribes of Israel.)

3) Leviticus 23:26 ff. "And *Hashem* spoke to Moses saying. **But** (אך) on the tenth day of the seventh month it is the day of atonement, a holy convocation it shall be for you ..."

Rashi comments here:

"The words אך and רק when they occur in the Torah have a limiting force—[here that would mean] the day atones only for those who do *tshuvah* (repent) **but** does not atone for those who do not do *tshuvah*."

4) Leviticus 23:39. "**But** (אך) on the fifteenth of the seventh month when you have gathered in the increase of the land you shall celebrate a festival unto *Hashem* seven days ..."

Rashi comments here:

"I might think [that the offering] should put aside [allow profaning] the Sabbath, therefore the Scripture says אך (limiting) because it has a supplementary period consisting of seven days [when it can also be offered and thus should not be done on the Sabbath.]"

5) Exodus 31:13. (this is our verse) "**But** (אך) My Sabbaths you should observe because it is a sign between Me and you that I *Hashem* have sanctified you."

The Talmud learns from our verse: "**But** My Sabbaths you should observe.." that the Sabbath may be violated to save a life (*pikuach nefesh*). That is, the word אך "but" limits the observance of the Sabbath.

Two Different uses of אך

Look closely at these five examples and place them in two separate groups according to their use of the word אך.

Your Answer:

An Answer:

> *Group I.* Examples 1) and 2) have the word אך limiting the statement in the *previous* phrase.

> *Group II.* Examples 3), 4), and 5) have the word אך limiting the words *following* it.

Another difference is:

> *Group I.* The meaning of "But" is used in the normal, common sense way. We normally make statements and then qualify what has been said with the words "but", "however", or "nevertheless." In examples 1) and 2) above אך is used in its Plain Sense, in the *p'shat* sense.

> *Group II.* The meaning of "but" is used in a way that is not based on common sense usage. To say, for example, that אך restricts the Shabbath for *pikuach nefesh*, is reasonable from a *halachic* point of view, but certainly cannot be considered the *p'shat* in the verse. This is a *drash* interpretation.

P'SHAT AND DRASH IN TORAH INTERPRETATION _____

A basic difference between *p'shat* and *drash* interpretation in the Torah is that *p'shat* must make sense within the context in which it is found. *Drash*, on the other hand, is not bound by the context and it may introduce ideas or characters that are in no way hinted at in the text. As an example, the *midrash* says that when Jacob blessed Ephraim and Menashe (Genesis 48:16), he was also blessing Joshua bin Nun and Gideon. These individuals weren't even alive at the time of the blessings nor are they hinted at in the text. This must, therefore, be considered *drash*.

With this in mind, let us look at the two uses of the word אך in the Torah.

Group I uses the word אך in the *p'shat* mode of interpretation, in the common sense manner. In such cases the word always qualifies the words mentioned *before* it. In *Group II*, the word אך is interpreted in the *drash* mode, not the way it is used in common parlance. Then it limits the *mitzvah* that is referred to immediately *after* it. But, and this is crucial to understanding Rashi here, *in both cases, the word has a limiting effect: it qualifies some part of the verse.*

Now we can understand Rashi. He is telling us that אך qualifies and limits the building of the Tabernacle, because אך *always* limits. But here he is telling us the *p'shat* interpretation of אך. The Ramban, it seems, took Rashi to mean that אך was to be understood as the Sages understood it, in the *drash* sense; and thus his attack on Rashi's comment.

SUPPORT FOR THIS EXPLANATION OF RASHI _____

Can we find evidence that Rashi, in fact, viewed the word אך in both a *p'shat* and a *drash* sense?

YOUR ANSWER:

An Answer: See Rashi's comment to Numbers 31:22. After the battle with Midian, the people are told to purify the plunder. First they were to purify the objects from a spiritual impurity. Afterwards, they were to cleanse the objects from their non-kosher elements. Rashi's comment on the purification of the gold and other objects is an excellent illustration of Rashi's awareness of the two different interpretations of the word אך, one *p'shat* and one *drash*.

"**Only the gold, etc.** *Rashi*: Although Moses did not warn you except for the laws of ritual uncleanliness, you must be warned further concerning the laws of purging. [Following is the *p'shat* interpretation of the word. A.B.] "Only" אך denotes limitation, as if to say, 'you are limited from using the utensils even after their purification from contamination by the dead, until they are purified from the absorption of forbidden meat, not ritually slaughtered. [Following comes Rashi's use of the *drash* interpretation. A.B.] Our Rabbis remarked in *drash* that "only the gold" teaches that one must remove its rust before purging it. This is the connotation of the word אך, there should be no rust there only the metal, exactly as it is."

This is a striking example of Rashi's attention to the two uses of interpretation of the word אך. Notice how the first interpretation of אך, which is *p'shat*, limits the *previous* discussion of ritual uncleanliness, i.e., the ritual purification is not yet enough to permit one to use the vessels, **but** you must also purge them from unkosher elements. The second interpretation of אך, which is *drash*, limits what comes next ("only the *gold*"). Only pure, not rusty, gold.

THE LESSON

Never underestimate Rashi's acumen. Stubborn persistence in our search for answers to apparent difficulties in Rashi, will only increase our appreciation of this astounding commentary.

(See *Gur Aryeh*)

Rashi's unique interpretation gives insight into the deeper meanings of the Sabbath.

Exodus 31:13

וְאַתָּה דַּבֵּר אֶל בְּנֵי יִשְׂרָאֵל לֵאמֹר אַךְ אֶת שַׁבְּתֹתַי תִּשְׁמֹרוּ כִּי אוֹת הִוא בֵּינִי וּבֵינֵיכֶם לְדֹרֹתֵיכֶם לָדַעַת כִּי אֲנִי הֹ' מְקַדִּשְׁכֶם.

כִּי אוֹת הִיא בֵּתִי וּבֵתִיכֶם. אוֹת גְּדוֹלָה הִיא בֵּינֵינוּ שֶׁבָּחַרְתִּי בָּכֶם בְּהַנְחִילִי לָכֶם אֶת יוֹם מְנוּחָתִי לִמְנוּחָה.

For it is a sign between Me and you. *Rashi:* It is a great sign between us, that I have chosen you by letting you inherit for rest that day on which I rested.

Can you rephrase Rashi's comment in your own words?

What is he saying?

YOUR ANSWER:

WHAT IS RASHI SAYING? _____

Rashi is telling us that the sign here is not Sabbath, as it is usually interpreted to mean, rather the sign is "letting you inherit for rest the day on which I rested." That is to say: when Jews keep the Sabbath, this is a sign that G-d has chosen them.

This is certainly a novel interpretation of these words. What can you ask here?

YOUR QUESTION:

QUESTIONING RASHI _____

A Question: What forces Rashi to ignore the more likely interpretation: that Sabbath is the sign? Ordinarily we consider the Sabbath to be a sign that G-d created the world. Yet Rashi clearly doesn't say this. Why?

What's bothering him?

YOUR ANSWER:

WHAT IS BOTHERING RASHI? _____

An Answer: The beginning of this verse says: "You shall keep my Sabbaths" in
the plural. The words אות היא "*it is* a sign" on the other hand, are in
the singular. Therefore Rashi realized that "sign" cannot refer to
Sabbaths.

How does Rashi's comment avoid this difficulty?

YOUR ANSWER:

UNDERSTANDING RASHI _____

An Answer: The sign, according to Rashi, is the (singular) fact "that I have
chosen you to inherit My day of rest." This is a singular item and
thus the word "it" also in the singular, is grammatically appropriate.

Now, reread the whole section from 31:12 to 31:17. Do you see any redundancy
regarding the phrase "it is a sign"?

YOUR ANSWER:

A CLOSER LOOK _____

An Answer: See verse 17 where it says "Between Me and the Children of Israel
it is a sign forever..."

Why is this concept repeated?

Are there two signs here?

YOUR ANSWER:

An Answer: To answer this question, we must digress.

"KEEP" AND "REMEMBER" IN ONE UTTERANCE _____

The commandment of keeping the Sabbath is repeated in the two editions of the Ten Commandments in different ways. In the Book of Exodus (20:8 ff), it says:

"Remember the Sabbath day to sanctify it. Six days you may labor and do
all your work. But the seventh day is the Sabbath of *Hashem*, your G-d; do

not do any work, neither your son, nor your daughter, your servant, nor your maidservant, your beasts nor the stranger in your gates. For in six days *Hashem* made the heavens and the earth, the sea and all that is in them and rested on the seventh day; *therefore Hashem blessed the Sabbath day and sanctified it.*"

However, in the second Tablets (Deut. 5:12ff), we find a different reason given for the *mitzvah* of the Sabbath.

"Keep the Sabbath day to sanctify it, as *Hashem*, your G-d, has commanded you. Six days you may labor and do all your work. On the seventh day is the Sabbath of *Hashem* your G-d; don't do any work, neither you, nor your son, nor your daughter, your servant, nor your maidservant, nor any of your oxen, nor your ass, nor any of your animals, nor the stranger in your gates, in order that your servant and your maidservant may rest as well as you. And you shall remember that you were a servant in the land of Egypt and *Hashem* your G-d brought you out of there with a mighty hand and an outstretched arm; *therefore* Hashem *your G-d commanded you to keep the Sabbath day.*"

In the first Tablets, the reason given for the Sabbath is that G-d created the world in six days and rested on the seventh, while in the second Tablets, the reason given is that we were slaves in Egypt. This discrepancy has given rise to many attempts to reconcile it.

Can you answer it?

Your Answer:

An Answer: A close look at the Torah's words will reveal that there is no discrepancy whatsoever. In the first Tablets, it speaks of the creation and at the end it says: "Therefore *Hashem* blessed the Sabbath day and sanctified it." Meaning, the reason for the Sabbath is that it commemorates creation of the world by G-d.

In the second Tablets, it speaks of the Israelites' slavery and G-d's redemption of them. At the end it says: "therefore *Hashem* your G-d commanded *you* to keep the Sabbath day." Meaning, the reason the Jews, among all the nations of the earth, are commanded to keep the Sabbath (after all, it is a universal event, not exclusive to the Jews), is that we have a special indebtedness to G-d and He commanded us to proclaim His Divinity in the world.

In summary: There are two reasons for the Sabbath:
    1) The reason there is a Sabbath—the creation
    2) The reason the Jews alone are commanded to keep it—their redemption from Egypt.

Let us, now, return to our verses in *parashas Ki Sisa*.

Can you now see the significance of the repetition of the words "it is a sign between Me and you"?

Look carefully.

YOUR ANSWER:

A Deeper Look

The first verse (31:13): "It is a sign between Me and you for your generations, to know that I, *Hashem*, have made you holy."

The second verse (31:17): "Between Me and the Children of Israel it is an everlasting sign, that *Hashem* made the heavens and the earth in six days and on the seventh day He ceased and rested."

Which verse corresponds to the reason in the first Tablets?

Which, to the reason in the second Tablets?

YOUR ANSWER:

Of course, the first verse ("that I, *Hashem*, made you holy") corresponds to the reason in the second Tablets (that Israel alone was chosen to keep the Sabbath) and the second verse ("that *Hashem* made the heavens and the earth") corrresponds exactly to the reason given in the first Tablets (that G-d created the heavens and the earth). Amazing how precise the Torah is in its choice of words!

Remember, it was Rashi's unusual interpretation of the first verse (31:13) that started us on this journey, by telling us that the sign is meant to signify the connection between G-d and His people. Not so the second time the sign is mentioned in verse 17; there it symbolizes the creation of the world by the Almighty.

SUBTLETIES OF THE TEXT

Do you see another subtlety in the text that substantiates the difference between the two verses?

Look very closely!

YOUR ANSWER:

An Answer: The first verse, which speaks of G-d's special relationship with His people, is written in the more personal, second person—"Between Me and *you*....who makes *you* holy."

The second verse which tells of G-d's lofty, supernatural powers as the Creator is written in the impersonal, third person—"Between Me and the Children of Israel." This form is used, it would seem, because a person cannot have a personal relationship with G-d as Creator. We can, on the other hand, have such a relationship with G-d as our personal redeemer. The choice of words in each phrase reflects precisely its deeper meaning.

The Torah nevers ceases to amaze one by its precise and subtle use of words.

THE LESSON

No matter how familiar you are with the Torah *parashah*, search it again and again to find its hidden treasures.

(See *Sefer Zikaron; Ho'el Moshe*)

Rashi has been known to answer several questions with the addition of a word or two. Here is an example of that.

Exodus 35: 4

וַיֹּאמֶר מֹשֶׁה אֶל כָּל עֲדַת בְּנֵי יִשְׂרָאֵל לֵאמֹר זֶה הַדָּבָר אֲשֶׁר צִוָּה הי לֵאמֹר.

> **זה הדבר אשר צוה ה':** לי **לאמר** לכם.
> **This is the word that Hashem commanded:** *Rashi*: Me **to say** to you.

Notice how Rashi inserts just a few words into the body of the verse. (The words in bold letters are the Torah's words.)

QUESTIONING RASHI

What would you ask here?

YOUR QUESTION:

A Question: This looks like a Type II Rashi-comment, one that helps us avoid a misunderstanding.

What misunderstanding is Rashi helping us avoid?

YOUR ANSWER:

WHAT MISUNDERSTANDING IS RASHI HELPING US AVOID?

An Answer: Did you notice that the word לאמר is used twice in this verse?

The word לאמר can be translated in one of two ways.

1) Its usual meaning is: "Saying," as in "G-d spoke to Moses saying." It is similar to quotation marks in our modern way of writing.

— 191

2) Another, rarer, meaning is "to tell to," or "saying to" as in

וַיְדַבֵּר הי אֶל מֹשֶׁה וְאֶל אַהֲרֹן לֵאמֹר אֲלֵהֶם.

And *Hashem* spoke to Moses and Aaron **to tell** them.
(Leviticus 11:1)

Rashi is clarifying that the second לאמר in our verse means "to tell to." It does not have its usual meaning of "saying," as does the first לאמר in the verse.

But how does Rashi know that this is its meaning here?

Hint:

Look above at verse 25:2 (beginning of *parashas Terumah*) where G-d first commanded regarding contributions to the Tabernacle. Our verse is a recounting of that original command.

YOUR ANSWER:

UNDERSTANDING RASHI

An Answer: In Exodus 25:2 it says "*Hashem* spoke to Moses *saying*: Speak to the Children of Israel and ***they*** **should take** for Me an offering etc." But our verse says "**Take from** *you* an offering..." Note that our verse has Moses speaking directly to the people; he is not quoting *Hashem*. This is how Rashi knows that לאמר here means "to tell to them," and is not a quote from G-d.

A CLOSER LOOK

But if we look closely at Rashi's comment we see that he not only adds the words "tell them" he also adds the word "commanded **me**." Why does he?

Hint:

Compare our verse with verse 35:1 above.

YOUR ANSWER:

An Answer: In verse 35:1 it says "These are the words that *Hashem* commanded etc." Why, then, does the Torah repeat again in our verse "This is the word that *Hashem* commanded to say."If you can answer this question you will have understood why Rashi adds the word "me."

Can you think of an answer?

YOUR ANSWER:

An Answer: The command above was to keep the Sabbath; Moses himself was also commanded to observe this *mitzvah*. Therefore it *does not* say "These are the words that *Hashem* commanded **to say** to them." However our verse is a command to the Children of Israel but not to Moses, therefore it includes the word לאמר "say to them." This is why Rashi stresses "G-d commanded **me... to tell you.**" G-d did not command Moses to contribute, but He did command Moses *to tell* the Israelites to contribute to the Tabernacle.

A Lesson

With a minimum of words Rashi can answer a bundle of questions. Pay attention to each one of his words.

(SEE *Liphshuto shel Rashi*)

A Type II comment meant to dispel any misunderstanding.

Exodus 35:23

וְכָל אִישׁ אֲשֶׁר נִמְצָא אִתּוֹ תְּכֵלֶת וְאַרְגָּמָן וְתוֹלַעַת שָׁנִי וְשֵׁשׁ וְעִזִּים
וְעֹרֹת אֵלִים מְאָדָּמִים וְעֹרֹת תְּחָשִׁים הֵבִיאוּ.

וכל איש אשר נמצא אתו: תכלת או ארגמן או תולעת שני או
עורות אילים או תחשים כולם הביאו.

And every man with whom it was found: *Rashi:* **turquoise wool** or **purple wool** or **scarlet wool** or **rams' skins** or *techashim* — they all **brought.**

What is Rashi Saying ?

This appears to be a Type II Rashi-comment. Rashi inserts his words into the Torah's words. Which words does he add?

YOUR ANSWER:

An Answer: Rashi makes two additions:

> 1) adds the word אוֹ "or" between the names of the various materials.
>
> 2) adds the word כולם "they all" before the word "they brought."

Why does he do this? What misunderstanding might we make?

YOUR ANSWER:

A Possible Misunderstanding

An Answer: The verse in the Torah says "And every man with whom was found blue purple *and* red purple *and* etc." I might have thought that a person had to possess all the items mentioned in order to be allowed to contribute, because each item begins with a ו "and."

How does Rashi avoid this misunderstanding?

YOUR ANSWER:

Understanding Rashi

By inserting the word "or," Rashi clarifies the point that the ו means "or" and not "and," thus a person could contribute even if he possessed only one of the items enumerated.

A Closer Look

The reason for Rashi's addition of the word כולם is more subtle. The verse begins in the singular "And *every* man with whom was found etc." yet ends with the plural word הביאו "*they* brought." Rashi reconciles this inconsistency by adding the word כולם "they all," meaning that while each individual brought his item, all these added up to the plural "they brought."

Exodus 35:34

וּלְהוֹרֹת נָתַן בְּלִבּוֹ הוּא וְאָהֳלִיאָב בֶּן אֲחִיסָמָךְ לְמַטֵּה דָן.

וְאָהֳלִיאָב: משבט דן מן הירודים שבשבטים מבני השפחות והשוווהו המקום לבצלאל למלאכת המשכן והוא מגדולי השבטים לקיים מה שנאמר "ולא נכר שוע לפני דל (איוב לד: יט).

And Ahaliav: *Rashi*: [He] was from the tribe of Dan, of the lowliest among the Tribes, one of the sons of the maid-servants, yet G-d equates him to Bezalel in the work of the Tabernacle, who was from the greatest of the tribes. This exemplifies what it says (Job 34:19) "He does not recognize the wealthy over the poor."

WHAT IS RASHI SAYING ?

Rashi's message is clear. He says that Torah teaches us a moral lesson, i.e. that G-d does not show preference to the privileged over the less privileged. We derive this from the fact that G-d chose Ahaliav, the son of one of Jacob's maidservants, to be on an equal footing with Bezalel, the son of Leah, one of Jacob's wives, in the holy work of constructing the Tabernacle. And we are made aware of this by the phrasing of our verse.

But when we compare our verse with a previous one, we have a question. See 31:6 (*parashas Ki Sisa*). There it says:

וַאֲנִי הִנֵּה נָתַתִּי אִתּוֹ אֵת אָהֳלִיאָב בֶּן אֲחִיסָמָךְ לְמַטֵּה דָן וגו'.

"I have given with him (Bezalel) Ahaliav the son of Achisamach of the Tribe of Dan, etc."

QUESTIONING RASHI

A Question: On the above words Rashi has no comment. Why didn't he make the comment he made on our verse, on this earlier verse? This verse also mentions Ahaliav together with Bezalel.

> *Hint*:

Compare the wording of the two verses.

YOUR ANSWER:

UNDERSTANDING RASHI

An Answer: In verse 31:6 it says "with him (Bezalel.)" The word "with" can be understood to mean "subordinate to" and not necessarily "equal to." While in our verse we have the words "him and Ahaliav etc." Here the two are placed on an equal basis. Thus it is not by chance that Rashi makes his comment here and not earlier; only here does the wording of the verse stress their equality.

LESSON

It is always wise to assume that Rashi will make an appropriate comment at the earliest opportunity in the Torah. If he does not, then we must strive to understand why.

Another of those short interspersed comments. What does it teach us?

Exodus 39:32

וַתֵּכֶל כָּל עֲבֹדַת מִשְׁכַּן אֹהֶל מוֹעֵד וַיַּעֲשׂוּ בְּנֵי יִשְׂרָאֵל כְּכֹל אֲשֶׁר צִוָּה ה' אֶת מֹשֶׁה כֵּן עָשׂוּ.

> **ויעשו בני ישראל.** את המלאכה **ככל אשר צוה ה' וגו'.**
> **And the Children of Israel made**: *Rashi*: the work ac-
> cording to all that *Hashem* commanded etc.

WHAT IS RASHI SAYING?

Rashi adds just the two words, "the work." He is telling us that the Israelites did the work (of the Tabernacle). You certainly have a question on
that!

YOUR QUESTION:

QUESTIONING RASHI

A Question: What has Rashi told us that we didn't know before? Of course the
verse is telling us that the Children of Israel did the work. That is
what the first half of the verse says, "And all the work of the Tabernacle was finished..."

What is Rashi adding to our understanding? Notice that this comment has the Type II style, meaning there is a possible misunderstanding here.

What misunderstanding?

Hint:

There is also a problem which is bothering Rashi here.

See the whole verse.

Your Answer:

What Misunderstanding? — What is Bothering Rashi? _____

An Answer: Did you notice that the word "to do" is repeated in this verse?

> "And the Children of Israel **did** all that *Hashem* commanded Moses, so they **did**."

This repetition of the word "did" is what is bothering Rashi.

How does his comment solve this problem?

Your Answer:

Understanding Rashi _____

An Answer: By adding the words "the work" Rashi deftly accomplishes two things.

First, he clarifies a possible misunderstanding. He tells us that the word ויעשו means "to make" and not "to do." They *made* the work (meaning, the Tabernacle and the vessels).

Secondly, he shows us that there is no repetition here. The verse is to be read as two separate clauses. It now reads "And the Children of Israel made (the Tabernacle). Just as *Hashem* had commanded Moses so they did."

(See Silbermann)

A Closer Look _____

Rashi adds the words את המלאכה in his comment.

Do you have a question here?

Hint:

Compare these words of Rashi to the words in the beginning of this verse.

What do you see? Do you see anything strange?

Your Answer:

An Answer: The Torah uses the words עבודת המשכן. Rashi uses the words את המלאכה.

Why does Rashi say מלאכה when the Torah says עבודה?

Hint:

See verses 39: 42-43

YOUR ANSWER:

A BETTER UNDERSTANDING

An Answer: Though most English translations translate both these words as "work," this is imprecise. The word עבודה means "work" in the sense of labor or toil. It has the meaning of an activity. The word מלאכה, on the other hand, means the product of that labor; the artifact created. This is how the words are used in verses 39:42-43.

In view of our understanding of Rashi's comment, i.e. that he is telling us that the word ויעשו means "to make," then the word מלאכה is appropriate and not the word עבודה.

One *makes* an artifact, and one *does* work. But one doesn't *do* an artifact, nor does one *make* labor.

A LESSON

Rashi's verbal precision is amazing; his choice of words must always be an object of study.

(See Leibowitz, *Eyunim, Shemos pg. 494*)

A famous drash which still needs to be analyzed.

Exodus 40: 35

וְלֹא יָכֹל מֹשֶׁה לָבוֹא אֶל אֹהֶל מוֹעֵד כִּי שָׁכַן עָלָיו הֶעָנָן וּכְבוֹד ה'
מָלֵא אֶת הַמִּשְׁכָּן.

וְלֹא יָכֹל מֹשֶׁה לָבוֹא אֶל אֹהֶל מוֹעֵד. וכתוב אחד אומר "ובבא
משה אל אהל מועד" בא הכתוב השלישי והכריע ביניהם, "כי
שכן עליו הענן," אמור מעתה כל זמן שהיה עליו הענן לא היה
יכול לבא, נסלק הענן נכנס ומדבר עמו.

Moses was unable to enter the Tent of Meeting: *Rashi*:
Yet another verse states:"And when Moses would come
into the Tent of Meeting (Numbers 7:89)." [This is an
apparent contradiction.] There comes a third verse [the
continuation of our verse] and reconciles them : "for the
cloud rested on it (the Tent of Meeting)." We can conclude then that as long as the cloud was upon it he could
not come in; but once the cloud left, he would enter and
speak with Him.

WHAT IS RASHI SAYING?

Rashi deals with an apparent contradiction between our verse which
says that Moses could not enter the Tent and another verse in The Book
of Numbers where it clearly states that Moses *did* enter the Tent to speak
with G-d. The contradiction is easily resolved by a deduction made from
the words of the last part of our verse. There it says "because the cloud
rested on it." Thus the reason for Moses' being prevented from entering
the Tent was because of the cloud that filled it. A logical inference is that
when the cloud was not there, Moses could enter the Tent. This, then,
resolves, the contradiction.

This method of resolving apparent contradictions is one of Rav
Yishmael's Thirteen Principles of *midrashic* interpretation. The principle states: When you have two contradictory verses, then a third verse
is cited to reconcile the contradiction. We recite Rav Yishmael's Thirteen Principles every day in the beginning of the morning prayers.

With all due respect to this principle of Rav Yishmael, we must still ask
questions in order to understand it fully.

What would you ask?

Hint:

Remember Rashi said that *Hashem* spoke to Moses when the cloud lifted. Now look at the next verse, Exodus 40:36. "And when the cloud lifted from upon the Tabernacle, the Children of Israel traveled, on all their travels."

What would you ask?

YOUR QUESTION:

QUESTIONING THE *DRASH*

A Question: If G-d only spoke to Moses when the cloud lifted; and if the people journeyed as soon as the cloud lifted, when was there time for G-d to speak to Moses?

Can you think of an explanation?

YOUR ANSWER:

SOME POSSIBLE EXPLANATIONS

An Answer: The Rashbam explains that the cloud was lifted from covering the Tabernacle *in toto* (that is why Moses could not enter) and then it rested above the Cheribum, in the Holy of Holies, until the time for journeying. So Moses was prevented from entering only when the cloud filled the whole Tabernacle, but not when it was hovering above the Ark and the Cheribum in the Holy of Holies.

Another answer given is that the cloud covered the Tent of Meeting only for a short period of time, an hour or so, afterwards it lifted. That is when Moses could enter and communicate with G-d. This is hinted at in the words:

$$\text{כי שָׁכַן עָלָיו הֶעָנָן}$$

See how the first letters of these words spell the word שעה "hour."

THE RAMBAN'S VIEW

The Ramban explains the Sages' view and offers a *p'shat* interpretation as well.

He says that when it says that Moses could not enter, it means he was not permitted to enter without G-d calling him. He could enter, however, if G-d called to him. (As we find in the very first verse of the Book of Leviticus, which comes immediately after our verses.)

The Ramban writes:

> "According to the *p'shat* of the verse, since it says 'And *Hashem* spoke to him *from* the Tent of Meeting.' Moses did not enter the Tabernacle, rather *Hashem* called to him from the Tent of Meeting and he stood at the entrance of the Tent of Meeting and He spoke with him."

Note that with this *p'shat* interpretation of the verses, there is no contradiction between them. One verse relates to the times that Moses was called by G-d and thus *could* enter, or more specifically, could stand at the entrance; the other verse, relates when he was not called and, therefore, *could not* enter.

The Ramban also explains the *drash* of the Sages (as quoted in Rashi). The *drash*, he says, was based on the assumption that Moses could enter the Tent of Meeting whenever he wanted to, without being called by G-d. As a result of this view, the verse "And when Moses came into the Tent etc." seems to contradict our verse, which says that Moses could not enter. The Ramban explains the Sages' view:

> "This (Moses entering at will, the verse in Numbers 7:89 'And when Moses would come etc.') was only after the cloud no longer covered the whole tent (but remained only over part of it, as the Rashbam above). And this was only on the eighth day of the Dedication ceremonies. But the "calling" which is referred to in the verse 'And He called to Moses and He spoke to him from the Tent of Meeting' (Leviticus 1:1) took place before this (on the first day of Dedication)."

What Is the Ramban Saying?

In summary: The Ramban says the Sages' view was that Moses was always allowed to enter without Divine permission. But only on the first day of Dedication was it necessary for G-d to call him because of Moses' fear of entering the Tent, it being such a holy place. Thus the verse in Numbers 7:89, "And when Moses would come," refers the usual situation when Moses could enter at will. The verse in the beginning of Leviticus, "And He called to Moses and *Hashem* spoke to him from the

Tent of Meeting," refers to the unique situation on the first day of the Dedication. And our verse, "And Moses could not enter (without permission)," refers to the final day of Dedication when the cloud covered the whole Tabernacle and Moses could not enter at all.

The Ramban's own *p'shat* interpretation removes the contradiction to begin with, by assuming that Moses could come to the entrance of the Tent only with permission. When the Torah says he could not enter, that is because G-d did not give him permission.

We see again how the Ramban offers both a *p'shat* interpretation as well as interpreting the Sages' *drash* interpretation. This is something he does frequently in his commentary.

(See Tov Yerushalyim)

Appendix

A possible solution to the Rashi Tabernacle column brainteaser (see page 159).

Diagram C — *Maaseh Choshev*'s solution.

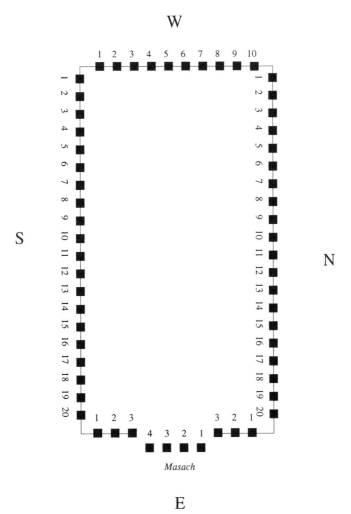

Note: There are no corner columns. They are set back 2 ¹/₂ cubits from the ends. This arrangement solves all the problems. However, we must interpret Rashi's statement that there were 5 cubits "between the column at the end of the southern row, standing at the Southeast corner, to the [first] column which was one of the three in the East." We must now interpret this to mean that there were 5 cubits of *curtain* between these columns: 2 $1/2$ at the end of the South side and 2 $1/2$ at the beginning of the East side. Actually the verse itself *is* talking about curtains, so this is a reasonable interpretation.

Lesson

We must admit that the above suggested solution is not "perfect." But it is the best I could find. We can be confident that, were Rashi here to ask, he would offer an explanation that would be "problem-free." It is our task to continue to search for it.

The following people have made the publication of this book possible:

Dr. & Mrs. Marvin Blush
Moshe & Shushu HarShemesh
Jordan & Vivian Lurie
Marv Silverman
Mil Rothschild
Mitch & Rachel Rothschild

Their generosity is gratefully acknowledged.

About the Author

Avigdor Bonchek has Rabbinic ordination from Ner Israel Rabbinical College of Baltimore and a doctorate in clinical psychology from New York University. He has taught Torah studies at the Ohr Somyach Center for Judaic Studies in Jerusalem. He has been a lecturer of psychological courses at the Hebrew University of Jerusalem for the past 25 years. Previously he taught at the City University of New York, Yeshiva University and Ben Gurion University in Israel. Dr. Bonchek is a practicing psychotherapist. His book *The Problem Student: A Cognitive/Behavioral Approach* has been published in Hebrew. His book *Studying the Torah: A Guide to In-Depth Interpretation* has been published by Jason Aronson Publishers. Dr. Bonchek lives in Jerusalem with his wife, Shulamis, and their six children.